Lewis & Clark In The Bitterroot

— BY THE DISCOVERY WRITERS —
- Jeanne O'Neill
- Jean Clary
- Patricia B. Hastings
- Diann Ladd
- Katie White
- Riga Winthrop

With a Foreword by Dale A. Burk

Lewis & Clark In The Bitterroot

— BY THE DISCOVERY WRITERS —

- Jeanne O'Neill
- Jean Clary
- Patricia B. Hastings
- Diann Ladd
- Katie White
- Riga Winthrop

With a Foreword by Dale A. Burk

Copyright 1998 by Dale A. Burk

First Printing, November 1998
Second Printing, December 1998

ISBN 0-912299-71-1 (softcover)
ISBN 0-912299-76-2 (hardcover)

Library of Congress Catalog Card Number: 98-61483

STONEYDALE PRESS PUBLISHING COMPANY
523 Main Street • P.O. Box 188
Stevensville, Montana 59870
Phone: 406-777-2729

TABLE OF CONTENTS

Unless otherwise noted, chapters were written by Jeanne O'Neill.

DEDICATION

Dr. Gene Swanzey (left) with Gary Moulton on the top of Saddle Mountain, Bitterroot Range, Montana. (Photo by John Irving Stroud)

THIS BOOK IS FONDLY DEDICATED TO

DR. GENE SWANZEY

Who made himself and his library available, who shared knowledge and humor, wisdom and common sense, and placed six naive writers in the context of the Corps of Discovery as they transversed the Bitterroot Valley and Mountains in 1805 and 1806. In so doing, Dr. Swanzey became the seventh member of The Discovery Writers.

ACKNOWLEDGEMENTS

Our appreciation to:

•*Dale Burk, our editor and publisher, who suggested the idea for this book, nurtured the project and believed in us even when we doubted.*

•*Dr. Gene Swanzey, our mentor and friend, who opened his library and also his heart to us, and steered us in the right direction with wisdom, humor and meticulous adherence to the facts.*

•*Mary Ann Swanzey who graciously welcomed us into her home.*

•*Stephen Ambrose, author of "Undaunted Courage," who on a visit to the Bitterroot encouraged us to proceed with this effort.*

•*Gary Moulton, whose encouragement has been an inspiration to all of us.*

•*Our families and friends, particularly our husbands, for their patience, support and encouragement.*

•*Tony Incashola, director of the Salish Culture Committee, and Thompson R. Smith, ethnohistorian, the Salish Culture Committee Staff, and the Elders' Advisory Council of the Confederated Salish and Kootenai Tribes for their assistance with the Salish people's perspective of their encounter with the Corps of Discovery.*

•*Ginny Mellgren for recruiting reference material.*

•*Shirley and Phil Althen for their generosity in allowing us access to their Lewis and Clark files.*

•*Dr. Robert Bergantino for his professional assistance in reading maps and locating campsites.*

•*The staff of North Valley Library in Stevensville: Patty Jo Thomas, Bill Stout and Ellie Scrivner for their cooperation and assistance in locating references.*

•*Virginia Todd, our former member, for providing the Gary Moulton edition of the Lewis and Clark Journals to the North Valley Public Library*

•*Ed Hastings for his photos and for plodding along with us over forest trails in the Bitterroot.*

•*Pat and Ernie Deschamps for their cordial welcome into their home and on their land, the proposed Traveller's Rest site at Lolo, Montana.*

•*Joe Mussulman for sharing his knowledge and experience in publishing.*

•*Dr. Ronald V. Loge for contributing information on the medicines used by Captains Lewis and Clark.*

•*Vern Sylvester for guidance in ascertaining the geography of the Bitterroots.*

•*Judy Allen and the Bitterroot Writers for listening and suggesting.*

•*The Traveller's Rest Chapter of the Lewis and Clark Trail Heritage Foundation for their generous support and encouragement.*

•*George Knapp and Chuck Sundstrom for their presentation of the Traveling Trunk.*

•*Chuck Campbell for his insights and explanations in regard to the trail taken by the Expedition.*

•*Fern Hart, Art Garner, and Laura Millen for their assistance in getting pictures of the Paxson murals.*

•*Jan Williamson and Billie Linkletter of Stoneydale Press for their patience and availability.*

•*Mary C. Horstman, forest historian for the Bitterroot National Forest Service, for sharing information and explaining the role of the Forest Service in preserving historic sites.*

•*Carolynne Merrell for her insights as avocational archeologist.*

•*Judy Wohlert of the National Park Service, Spaulding, Idaho*

•*Marsha Wattnem of Stevensville for her assistance on the computer.*

•*Robert F. Morgan of Helena, Montana, Joe Thornbrugh of Victor, Montana, and Elmer Sprunger of Bigfork, Montana, for their incredible paintings reproduced in this book.*

•*Kirby Lambert, curator, and Diane Keller of the Montana Historical Society in Helena, Montana.*

•*Diana J. Tasker, director of the Clymer Museum of Art in Ellensburg, Washington.*

•*Bozeman Library for use of materials in this book.*

•*Any person not mentioned who contributed in any way to the publication of "Lewis and Clark in the Bitterroot," be it a word of encouragement, a clipping from the newspaper, a question or a pat on the back. We thank you.*

•*And particularly to the members of our Scripture Study Group who supported and encouraged us, shared our venture, listened patiently and most important, prayed with us. Many thanks.*

FOREWORD

No SINGLE EPISODE in American history holds as powerful or enduring a place in its people's imagination, whether that perception comes from fact or fancy, as the first major exploratory expedition sent out in the nation's name — the Lewis and Clark Expedition. And no wonder! Two inescapable aspects of the journey worked from the time of the expedition, in the early part of the 1800s, to this day to create and constantly embellish a romantic legend that places this exploratory journey among the most incredible of all history, not just American history.

The first was that the Corps of Discovery, the expedition's official name given it by its originator, President Thomas Jefferson, made it. Its mission, if not its hope of finding an easy water-based route to the Pacific, was accomplished in the face of both doubt and difficulties of the time. Secondly, and most incredible given the circumstances of constant daily peril for this group of military personnel in hostile and largely unknown territory, not one member of the Corps of Discovery was lost to accident, enemies, injury or climatic harshness, though all those factors were encountered time and again on the trip. And one, only one, member of the contingent perished on the trip, Sergeant Charles Floyd, of what was apparently an appendicitis attack. Further, that particular ailment would have killed him in those days had he come down with it across the street from a hospital in one of the nation's larger cities.

Beyond that, both for their contemporaries and for those of us who have come on the American scene since, the Lewis and Clark Expedition, by accomplishing its task, established a tone of continental consciousness among Americans of that and all subsequent generations. And it literally unleashed an unquenchable spirit of a nation to embrace an entire continent, from the Atlantic to the Pacific where Captain William Clark carved, into a pine tree, a notation of their triumph: "William Clark December 3rd 1805. By land from the U. States in 1804-1805."

We, the people of the United States, whether we know it or not, have lived in both the shadow and the tone of that triumphant moment ever since. Whether we're conscious of it or not, we as a people, exult with William Clark. His, their, accomplishment was, and is, ours. He and Meriwether Lewis might have led the expedition. Its toils, troubles, indeed its successes and exultations, were, in fact, theirs alone. But what they did, and how they did it, and why they did it, do not belong to them alone. They were there for us, for the United States of America of their time and for the United States of America of all subsequent time, for good or for bad. They achieved magnificent things and all of us, today, live in the legacy of that accomplishment. And while we don't NEED tangible proof of that achievement, it is regrettable that William Clark didn't carve that exultant affirmation of their success on a more enduring part of the landscape, instead of a tree, so it would be extent today like his carved signature on Pompey's Pillar in southeastern Montana. But maybe, just maybe, some things are more powerfully written in our minds and hearts than they can be written on a rock, or a tree. Maybe it doesn't matter that what he carved has, by natural process, disappeared into the labyrinth of time. What he carved is known to us, and that is what matters. It was a part of what William Clark and his compatriots experienced and felt; indeed, it's part of what we experience, when we ponder what he did, and wrote, and also who we are.

Certainly that is the case with most of the people I encounter who have even a minimal interest in the Lewis and Clark Expedition. It is not the cold fact and the remote recounting of their deeds that matter to most aficionados of the Expedition. It is for the passion that the men, and one woman, of the Corps of Discovery put into that journey to make it succeed. It is for the romance of the journey in the context of the difficult times in which the trip was made. And for the mystery of just how they did it, for even with the wonderful and detailed journals of the Expedition, even many known aspects of the trip remain shrouded in mystery and legend rather than hard, cold, undeniable fact. It is the wonderful, individual, personal, subjective evaluation of each aspect of the journey that allows, indeed dictates, its magic to us.

One astute and critical student, and I mean the word "critical" here in the context of a careful, thorough, studious pursuit of knowledge, of the Expedition's travels, Dr. Gene Swanzey of Hamilton, Montana, who believes that, often, it is what we read into what we know and observe about the Corps of Discovery that gives the Expedition its real power, its undeniable hold, over us. Dr. Swanzey has literally spent a lifetime devoted to the minutiae of the Corps' travels. On occasion, even when reading the journals on the exact spot where certain incidents occurred, he notes that it is difficult to determine exact locations, exact conditions because of climatological and environmental changes over the two centuries of natural processes since the Corps traveled through a specific area. Or to even imagine, in the comfort and conveniences of life nowadays, the Corps' hardship of continuing on, into the unknown, under conditions of almost unendurable labor, hunger, sometimes intense and gnawing hunger, even starvation, sickness, injury and deprivation.

On a recent field trip with a group of writers along a part of the Expedition's route through the Bitterroot Mountains, and the Bitterroot Valley in western Montana, without question some of the most difficult components of both the trip westward and the Corps' return journey in the spring of 1806, Dr. Swanzey might well have tapped the very root of why we Americans, nowadays at least, are so enthralled with the romance of the Lewis and Clark Expedition. First, it is OURS. It is inescapably American, written large and forever into our history and our hearts. Beyond that, simply because it is shrouded in mystery as to the exact details of its many parts and places, it is ours to interpret in an unending variety of ways, some correct and some undoubtedly incorrect. Second, as Dr. Swanzey has so insightfully concluded, after several decades of guiding touring parties of lay citizens, academics and writers alike to portions of the route of the Expedition, it is the very opportunity, and on some occasions the necessity, to speculate as to what route the Corps took in a certain area. Or to guess as to where they might have stopped for lunch in a certain area, or where they actually camped overnight. And further, to determine about where this incident or that occurred, that allows us to inject ourselves, wittingly or unwittingly, into a sense of participation in the process of the journey. Unlike the contemporary journeys of exploration where every detail of the route

The official Montana state statue commemorating the Lewis & Clark Expedition, by sculptor Robert Scriver, is located in Fort Benton, Montana. (Photo courtesy Dale A. Burk)

and process is known with almost exact preciseness, such as what we shared in a vicarious way with the space travel to the moon and back in the 1970s, comprehending many of the details of the Lewis and Clark Expedition is left, entirely, up to our imaginations. "Of course, we often must speculate about what really happened — where they camped, where they stopped to dine, what exact route they took. But if we couldn't speculate, it wouldn't be fun," Dr. Swanzey said. Indeed! Fun. Enjoyment. Pleasure. Excitement. Even transference. By speculating, by placing our interpretations upon what we read, and see, we are there, along with the Corps itself. In large part, the Lewis and Clark Expedition enthralls us as individuals, and as a people, because that very opportunity of speculation allows us to be a momentary, day-by-day, repetitive (and occasionally a correctable) participant in the process of discovery. It is, for sure, fun. And, often, a participation and understanding that we don't have to defend, even if we're partially or totally wrong in the conclusions we reach.

Take, for example, a perception of the Lewis and Clark Expedition that I grew up with, one grilled into me as a child by a grandmother born in the century in which the Expedition took place. Now she was a person born when women didn't have the vote but who nonetheless knew of the power of a woman to hold a family together in difficult times, of hard work, a woman raised in the remote farm country of Iowa near the fabled Missouri River. She came to the wilds of the upper Missouri River in Montana herself as a young child bride, a woman who at an early age and throughout her life read of the Lewis and Clark Expedition and purposely visited many places along the journey's route. An inveterate reader and a history buff, she became an unabashed champion of another young woman who she thought was the greatest heroine in American history, Sacajawea. It was my grandmother's deep conviction that the Expedition succeeded only because of Sacajawea, that this incredible young Shoshone Indian, like herself a diminutive woman, a mother with a newborn baby on her back, was at once the Expedition's guide and its unquestionable savior as it entered and passed through the land of the Blackfeet, Shoshone, Salish, Nez Perce and Crow. Never mind that I subsequently learned otherwise, that while Sacajawea unquestionably helped provide information and, in some circumstances such as at Beaverhead Rock in the uppermost reaches of the Missouri drainage provided certainty as to location, she did not "guide" the Expedition. Never mind, either, the intellectual concession that the Expedition most likely would have accomplished what it did even if Sacajawea had not been along. In a very real way, my grandmother was right. Her conviction of Sacajawea's greatness is unchallengeable. That conviction came out of my grandmother's inquiry into the Corps of Discovery, her speculation, her personal comprehension and understanding of this great episode in American history, in the history of HER land. And her personal hero, Sacajawea, who really had a powerful calming, peace-making impact, by her mere presence and upbeat personality, on the men of the Expedition and native peoples they met. And, as is often the case when speculation is a requirement of understanding, it is largely if not precisely correct. Sacajawea is still a larger-than-life character to me. In my lexicon of American heroes, she is in the highest category, and only part of that determination is a result of my grandmother's influence on me. Such determinations are, after all, personal and subjective. Any acquisition of knowledge and understanding, and difference of opinion from what my grandmother taught me I might have come to over the intervening years have not diminished one iota the respect and admiration I hold for that diminutive Shoshone woman. Whatever speculation we might undertake, whatever attributes or achievements we might give or take away from her don't change for a moment the fact that she *did* contribute vitally to the success of the Expedition and she was, and always will be, one of the greatest of American women.

Which brings us, finally, to the thrust of this book — a look at an incredibly significant, difficult, and often overlooked, even neglected, part of the Corps of Discovery's journey, its eventful and decisively important journey through the Bitterroot Mountains, and the Bitterroot Valley, in what now is known as western Montana and northcentral Idaho. The time that the Corps of Discovery spent in the Bitterroot had the potential, literally, to make or break the Expedition. They came into the headwaters of the Bitterroot Valley broken, wet and disheveled, cold, worn to the edge of despair, starving, their supplies running out or gone, under-horsed if they were to continue their journey across the Rockies. And they were only partially sure their old, hired Shoshone guide, Old Toby, could show them the way over the Lolo Trail into the land of the Nez Perce and direct access to the waters of the Pacific.

From the outset in this look at "Lewis and Clark in the Bitterroot," we learn that sometimes what is taken for fact is, in fact, not. For example, the Expedition didn't come over the mountains from the Lemhi into the Bitterroot over the piece of ground now known as Lost Trail Pass. They were west of that particular spot, at least three-quarters of a mile and perhaps more. In fact, as Dr. Swanzey is so emphatic to point out, no human-made trail of any kind existed in that place at that time so *there was no trail to be lost.* Further, it's doubtful that any member of the Expedition could have been, let alone might have been, in the snow and enshrouding fog, even a half-mile distant from the main party during the horrendously difficult time the entire Corps had in bringing its horses, and other provisions, over those mountains that day. On the day they crossed from the Lemhi into the Bitterroot, every member of the Expedition faced the reality, and unified responsibility, of their shared battle for survivability — an incredibly arduous task of bringing loaded, unshod horses up steep, snow-covered slopes in the face of an ongoing September blizzard, of maintaining their own treacherous footing under the loads they themselves carried, made it highly unlikely that any individual could, or would, have wandered away from the task at hand. There never was any such thing as a "Lost Trail Pass" insofar as the Lewis and Clark Expedition was concerned; the fact that such a name exists in and of itself speaks volumes to the notion of how easy it sometimes can be for speculation to lead us to conclusions, and aphorisms, that, while romantic in notion, are unquestionably false.

And some aspects of their sojourn through the Bitterroot are bigger than life. Most notable, of course, is that incredible scene immortalized by artist Charles M. Russell in his monumental painting "Lewis and Clark Meeting the Indians at Ross' Hole" written about elsewhere in this book and which adorns its front cover (and which, incidentally, is worth the trip to Helena, Montana, to see in its full splendor). These Indians were the Oot-la-shoots, the Salish, and while their initial reaction upon encountering the bedraggled members of the Corps of Discovery on that fateful September day of 1805 in that remote and beautiful basin in the upper Bitterroot was, according to tribal historians, initially one of suspicion and hostility, the stronger emotions of pity and concern prevailed. And, as they say, the rest is history. By the way, this volume presents the first-ever published version of that encounter from the Salish point-of-view, and you'll want to give that chapter particular attention. It's a fascinating perspective that provides us insight into this historically important moment from a long neglected viewpoint...

But, back to Ross' Hole in September of 1805, the Corps was replenished and refurbished, if not emotionally revitalized by a group of native people, the Salish, whom Expedition members themselves called the finest they had met on their entire journey. It traded for the horses it so desperately needed, and the Expedition was subsequently on its way through the Bitterroot Valley, to its significant stop(s) at Traveller's Rest at present-day Lolo, Montana, and on, once again through incredibly difficult circumstances, across the Bitterroot Mountains and on to the Pacific.

Twice the Corps of Discovery would be in the Bitterroot. Twice the time they spent there was significant in regard to the Expedition's success. Whether on the way west in the fall of 1805, when the question of the Expedition's potential to proceed to complete its westward journey was in doubt, or on its return journey in the spring of 1806 when a mood of triumphant and inevitable success marked the Corps' decisions, the Bitterroot is one of those places on the trail of the Lewis and Clark Expedition where fact and speculation come together in a most fascinating and powerful way.

It's a marvelous story, that of Lewis and Clark in the Bitterroot, in "these most terrible mountains I ever beheld" as Patrick Gass wrote in his journal at the time. Read on, and find out for yourself about Lewis and Clark in the Bitterroot, presented by the self-proclaimed "Discovery Writers" in thorough and solid detail in text, illustrations and photographs, true to what is known about the Corps of Discovery sojourn here .... but don't forget to speculate a bit as you do! There is, after all, fun in doing that however terrible the mountains might be, then or now. That is, after all, one undeniable fact that is as true today as it was when the Expedition made its way through the Bitterroot almost two hundred years ago...

Dale A. Burk
Stevensville, Montana
August 15, 1998

CHAPTER ONE

PRELUDE: FROM WASHINGTON, D.C. WESTWARD

THOMAS JEFFERSON, THIRD president of the fledgling United States of America, looked westward from his new home at 1600 Pennsylvania Avenue in Washington D.C. Once again he pondered the mysteries of that vast unknown land to the west, beyond the Mississippi River. This region, the Far West, extended to the Pacific Ocean and was not owned by the United States. Unexplored, uncharted, inhabited by a variety of indigenous peoples, yet unknown in Jefferson's civilized world, this virgin land beckoned for exploration, colonization and trade.

Already the fertile mind of Thomas Jefferson was forming another plan to send an expedition across this territory in the hope of finding a continental passage to the Pacific Ocean. Before he was president, Jefferson had planned two such expeditions, neither had materialized. However, a report by British trader, Alexander Mackenzie, confirmed Jefferson's fears: *the British were already beginning their own exploration inland from the western seacoast.* The advance of the powerful British threatened the territorial claims of this young nation and could disrupt its relations with the inland Indians and, perhaps, allow England to capture the lucrative fur trade.

Alongside Jefferson stood Meriwether Lewis, his young twenty-nine year-old secretary, hand-picked by the president himself, who described Lewis as "brave, prudent habituated to woods and familiar with Indian matters and character."[1] Lewis also shared with Jefferson an intense interest in natural science and was an eager pupil and observer in all that his employer taught him. In 1802 the

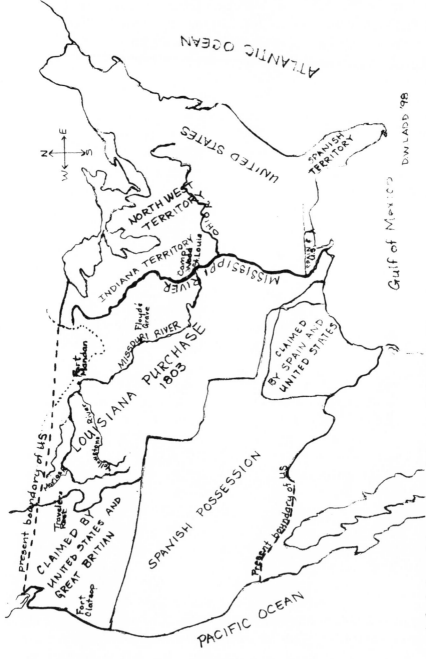

A depiction of the various claims to the land involving what is now the continental United States at the time of the Lewis and Clark Expedition.

President offered, and Lewis accepted, the leadership of an expedition to explore the Missouri River to its source and to seek a passage to the Pacific Ocean. President Jefferson also charged Lewis with the diplomatic mission of assuring the Indians they would encounter that the Great Father desired peace among the tribes, and in return he would send men with goods to trade and guns as well as ammunition. Assigned the rank of Captain in the U.S. Army, Lewis then invited his friend from Army days, William Clark, to join him. Clark was the younger brother of General George Rogers Clark, a friend of the President, who had once been approached by him to lead such an expedition, but the elder Clark had refused the offer. Together, Meriwether Lewis and William Clark chose and trained the men, mostly soldiers, a few civilians and French Canadian voyagers, who would accompany them. This military unit became known as the "Corps of Discovery."

However, Jefferson had to send diplomats to the Spanish to

"Lewis and Clark Expedition in 1804,' by Dean Cornwell (1892-1960). Oil on canvas, circa 1955. While the costumes and much of the equipment are not historically accurate in this painting, it sets a tone that reflects the Expedition's positive manner. Courtesy of the Montana Historical Society.

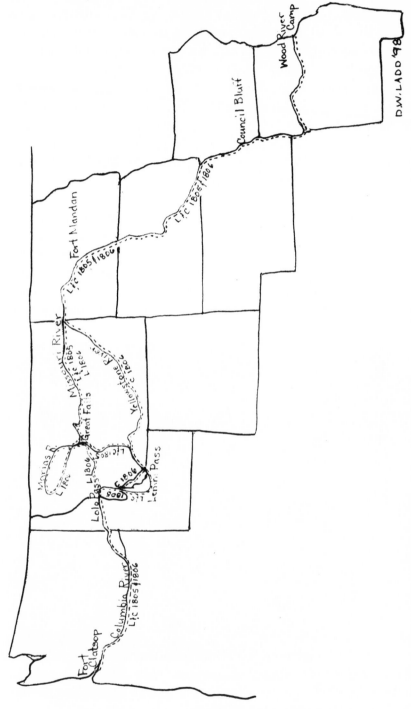

Lewis and Clark Expedition, 1805-06. Wood River Camp to Fort Clatsop, Fort Clatsop to Wood River Camp.

obtain passport into this Spanish Territory. The President then proceeded to use all his persuasive skills as statesman to convince Congress to authorize and to fund the expedition; it did, although quite meagerly, in early 1803. Lewis immediately began his preparations. Meanwhile, Spain had sold Louisiana to France. France's emperor, Napoleon, offered to sell this territory to the United States. President Jefferson seized the offer and acquired the Louisiana Purchase. Meriwether Lewis, William Clark and the Corps of Discovery were assured of traveling from the Mississippi to the Continental Divide through a wilderness which now belonged to the United States.

When Captain Lewis requested a captaincy rank for his friend and co-commander, William Clark, the Secretary of War issued, instead a second lieutenant rank to Clark. Lewis was frustrated but insisted that Clark be called captain and co-share the command and also that among the Corps of Discovery the matter be kept secret. Clark, although disappointed, agreed; so it was throughout the two-

"York," by Charles M. Russell. Watercolor, 1908. Scene in a Mandan village along the Missouri River during the upriver part of the journey. Courtesy of the Montana Historical Society.

"Lewis and Clark at Three Forks," by Edgar S. Paxson. Mural in the Montana State Capitol. Courtesy of the Montana Historical Society.

and-a-half-year journey — Captains Lewis and Clark.

On May 14, 1804, the Corps of Discovery, under the leadership of the co-captains, embarked from Camp Dubois across from the mouth of the Missouri River (in present-day Illinois). They proceeded up the Missouri to what is now North Dakota where they wintered at Fort Mandan with the Mandan and Hidatsa (Menetarees) Indians. Here they met and hired as translators Toussiant Charbonneau, a French trader, and his young pregnant Shoshone wife, Sacajawea or Sacagawea (which means "bird-woman" in Hidatsa). Five years earlier Sacajawea had been captured by the Hidatsa on a raid where the "three forks come together," what we now know was the three forks of the Missouri River in a remote part of the continent that would ultimately come to be known as Montana.

June, 1805. After traveling up the Missouri River, across North Dakota and present-day eastern Montana, the Corp arrived at the great falls of the Missouri. The men struggled through a laborious, even grueling portage around the falls and then continued up the river, but now the direction turned south. To the west the men saw the towering, snow-topped Rocky Mountains, higher, more rugged and impressive than any of them had ever seen before. Finally, on July 27, 1805, the Expedition arrived at the confluence, or forks of the three rivers, which Lewis and Clark named the Gallatin in honor of Secretary of the Treasury, Albert Gallatin; the Madison, honoring Secretary of State James Madison and the Jefferson, for the President. The captains chose to follow the larger and easy-flowing

Jefferson River westward. Sacajawea, now in familiar territory, soon recognized Beaver Rock, which is located near the present town of Dillon, Montana. Captain Lewis and three men pushed ahead of the main party and on August 12, 1805, they crossed the Continental Divide at Lemhi Pass, Idaho, the first white men to do so. The next day they met a band of Shoshone Indians which proved to be the same band to which Sacajawea had belonged. Subsequently, on August 17, 1805, Sacajawea was reunited with her people and, astonishingly, with her brother, the chief, Cameahwait. For six days in late August the members of the Expedition stayed with those very poor and starving Indians, whose only wealth was their horses, and who lived in constant fear of their enemies, the Blackfeet. It was not difficult for the captains to assure these impoverished natives that if they could obtain horses from them, which the Expedition desperately needed to cross the mountains, that the white men would help them by finding a direct way for the Shoshone to trade their furs for arms and other supplies for their comfort. Trading began, and the Expedition obtained enough horses to continue its journey.

The captains then gathered information through the translators, made maps and plotted their move over the mountains into the valley of the river, now named the Bitterroot. From there the captains planned to follow the trail which the Nez Perce Indians of Idaho used to cross the mountains to hunt buffalo, then onward to the Pacific Ocean. Thus the stage was set for the Corps of Discovery to enter the Bitterroot Valley and cross the Bitterroot Mountains on its journey westward, in September of 1805, and its return in June and July of 1806. The purpose of this book is to describe the presence of Lewis and Clark and the other members of the Expedition in the Bitterroots.

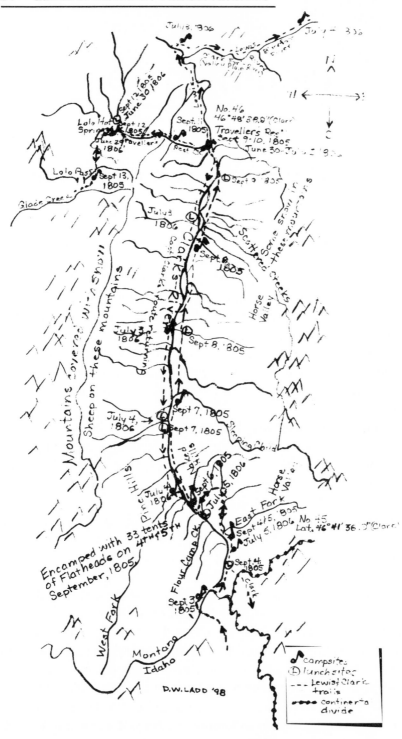

CHAPTER TWO

OVER THE BITTERROOT RANGE TO ROSS' HOLE

HUNGER GNAWED AT their bellies and the specter of starvation quivered through the weary and footsore men who followed their intrepid leaders, Captains Meriwether Lewis and William Clark, through the rugged Bitterroot Range of the Rocky Mountains during the first days of September 1805. By now the dream of finding an easy route to the Pacific Ocean had been shattered. Clark had explored the Salmon River leading south from the Shoshone camp and found it impassable. Their only way to the Pacific was to forge ahead across mountains and more mountains as far as they could see.

The men and Sacajawea had said farewell to her people, the Shoshone Indians, who themselves were about to leave and travel eastward on their annual buffalo hunt. The captains learned from the Shoshone that some distance to the north, beyond the arduous climb immediately before them, a trail existed which the Nez Perce took to cross the mountains on their way east to hunt buffalo. This same trail would lead the Corps of Discovery to the waters which flowed west to the Pacific.

By September 1, with twenty-nine pack horses obtained from the Shoshone, and, as Clark added, to *"Eate if necessary, "[1]* and with an old Shoshone guide whom they called Old Toby, plus Old Toby's son, the party headed north in search of the Nez Perce trail. Chief Cameahwait and Old Toby had warned the captains that there was no trail across the rugged mountains they now climbed. An easier way, they had been told, would be to go back to the Big Hole and once again cross back over the Continental Divide, and from there, through what is now known as Gibbon's Pass just a few miles south and then drop down into the valley of the Tushepau (Flathead) Indians. However, Lewis and Clark were not about to cross the Divide again, and they decided to force their way through these very inhospitable mountains, which are now, as they were then, heavily forested with pine and balsam and criss-crossed by creeks and ravines which slash through the steep mountainsides. To this day these mountain ranges, which form the boundary between Montana and Idaho, are still remote and rugged wilderness with few inhabitants. Thus began what has been described as *"the single most obscure and enigmatic of the entire Lewis and Clark expedition"*.[2]

Food was scarce. The Shoshones had been starving, existing only on fish and berries, not daring to cross into the territory of their enemies, the ferocious Blackfeet tribes, until hunger forced them to hunt the buffalo there. The Corps' hunters found little game in these mountains — a few grouse, an occasional deer. These hard-working frontiersmen, each accustomed to eating nine or ten pounds of meat a day, must have remembered and longed for the choice tongues and

On the Idaho side to the south of the Bitterroot Mountains, this sign notes that the Expedition made its way upward through the rugged and trail-less mountains toward what is now Montana.

livers of the abundant buffalo and elk venison the hunters had provided as the expedition crossed the plains. Provisions were giving out. Sergeant Ordway wrote *"nothing but a little parched corn to eat."[3]* Clark wrote on September 2, *"proceeded on thro' thickets in which we were obliged to Cut a road, over rockey hill Sides where our horses were in peteal (perpetual) danger of Slipping to their certain distruction & up & Down Steep hills, where Several horses fell, Some turned over, and others Sliped down Steep hill Sides, one horse Crippled & 2 gave out. With the greatest dificuelty risque &c. We made five miles & Encamped"[4].* On September 3 it snowed, about two inches, then rained, then sleet. Misfortune hit. The last thermometer was broken when one of the horses fell down a steep ravine. Clark wrote *"We passed over emence hils and Some of the worst roads that ever horses passed."[5]* From the journal of Joseph Whitehouse, *"Wed. 4th Sept. 1805, the morning clear but very cold. Our mockersons froze hard. The mountains covered with Snow...set out and assended a mountain without anything to eat....our fingers*

This is the route up which the party came from the Idaho side and then over the Bitterroot Range into Montana, except that when they made the climb the area was obscured by clouds and a vicious snowstorm. They followed the "defile" behind the ridge to the right. (Photo by Pat Hastings)

aked with the cold".[6] Their horses, although acclimated to the altitude and weather, labored with bruised feet. Some fell and rolled down the steep slopes, injuring themselves.

Dr. Gene Swanzey notes that "The Corps never did get near what is now called Lost Trail Pass. Most likely Old Toby implied a 'no way,' and the hunters spread out, desperately seeking game, and surely reported back to the party. Chief Cameahwait gave good advice on routes, and where no routes were possible. The Chief and Old Toby had implored Lewis to go where Gibbonsville now is and ascend Dahonolega Creek into the Big Hole to Trail Creek, and what later was called Clark's Pass, then to 'The Road to The Missouri' (Nee me poo) and Gibbon's Pass. The leaders chose not to go that way; thus the arduous trek up and over the mountains from the (now) Idaho side into the Bitterroot in (now) Montana. The people who for generations used the area encompassed by the pass the most didn't name it anything — they knew where it could lead them. Lost Trail Pass is a nice name except there was no trail to get lost. The party spent a miserable cold and hungry night of September 3, 1805, in those mountains. On the morning of September 4, once thawed out, they angled back below the highest point of Saddle Mountain to a low spot of the ridge line and descended to the dividing ridge between the East and West Forks of Camp Creek."

After thawing their frozen baggage these determined frontiersmen and their battered horses crossed over a ridge of Saddle Mountain through the snow and struggled on. Finally, the exhausted party wound its way down a ridge to the west fork of Camp Creek, which led to the river and into the valley at a meadow which was an Indian campground. Later this place was named Ross' Hole. Lewis named it, at the time, Clark's River. It is now the Bitterroot River. This particular spot on the East Fork of the Bitterroot River is not far from the present site of Sula.

Today powerful cars and trucks speed along U.S. Highway 93 through the Bitterroot Valley, traveling up and down the modern paved switchbacks which lead over the misnamed Lost Trail Pass. The highway passes over or near the routes and campsites where the men and Sacajawea battled their way through the wilderness on their tortuous passage through the mountains. A historical roadside sign

The Expedition came into Montana at the top or just behind the ridgetop at left in the top photo (literally the Bitterroot Mountain divide between Idaho and Montana) and then proceeded northward to the high, open ridge in the background, but still in a bitter snowstorm with vision extremely limited. They then went out toward Saddle Mountain in the background (bottom photo), wound their way down to the ridge in the foreground and followed it down into Camp Creek, and then took that drainage to Ross' Hole where they met up with the Salish. (Photos by Pat Hastings)

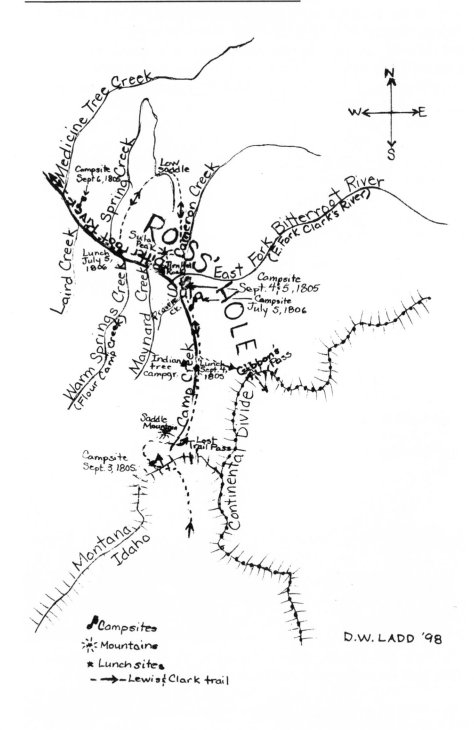

N
W← →E
S

Medicine Tree Creek

Low Saddle

Cameron Creek

East Fork Bitterroot River
(E. Fork Clarks River)

Campsite Sept 6, 1805

Spring Creek

Laird Creek

Sula Peak

Lunch July 5, 1806

Trail 1893

Warm Springs Creek
(Flour Camp Creek)

Maynard Creek

Camp Creek

ROSS' HOLE

Picaric ck.

Sula

Jim Hell Rock

Campsite Sept. 4, 5, 1805

Campsite July 5, 1806

Indian tree campgr.

Lunch Sept. 4, 1805

Gibbon's Pass

Saddle Mountain

Lost Trail Pass

Continental Divide

Campsite Sept. 3, 1805

Montana
Idaho

♪ Campsites
☼ Mountains
✱ Lunch sites
- → - Lewis & Clark trail

D.W. LADD '98

reminds travelers who care to stop that Lewis and Clark passed this way on September 4, 1805. In winter skiers enjoy both cross-country and downhill skiing over groomed slopes near where, nearly two-hundred years ago, horses fell and men struggled to right them and carry their baggage as they pursued their quest of a route to the Pacific Ocean. In summer, hikers, wearing sturdy boots with heavy treds on the soles, climb over sharp rocks and downed trees such as tore at the moccasins and bruised the feet of the members of the Lewis and Clark Expedition that first week in September, 1805.

Who were these men of the Corps of Discovery who suffered such hardships and yet persevered with their intrepid leaders through this wilderness? What of the two captains who inspired such loyalty and conviction in this group of rugged rough frontiersmen? How did the young Indian mother, Sacajawea, and her baby who accompanied them, fare through this journey? Were they the first white men to visit this land of the Bitterroots? What did they see? And why was

The Camp Creek drainage through which the Expedition came into Ross' Hole is in the background of this photo. The arrow points to the junction of the Camp Creek drainage with Ross' Hole, where the Corps encountered the Oot-la-shoot (Salish) Indians. (Photo by Pat Hastings)

the time they spent there so vital to the Expedition itself?

Another key point: Upon arrival in the Bitterroot, whom did they find? Fortunately for history and for us, both captains kept a journal of the Expedition and also requested their sergeants to do the same. From their accounts, written with pen and ink, sometimes under stressful circumstances after a hard day's march, we see the land, the rivers, the animals and birds, the cliffs, prairies, and forests as they existed in pristine condition before the westward march of "progress" changed the landscape forever.

CHAPTER THREE

MEMBERS OF THE EXPEDITION

Wアアア HAT SORT OF men were those who came over the mountains on that incredibly arduous journey into the upper reaches of the Bitterroot and thereby, upon meeting with the Ootlashoots (Salish) people there, make this spot hallowed ground in the annals of American history? Certainly the mere fact that they'd made it to this point, to what we now call Ross' Hole on the East Fork of the Bitterroot River, gives insight into both their perseverance and the depth of their character. Beyond that, what ensued in that incredible scene immortalized in the painting by Charles M. Russell of Lewis and Clark meeting the Indians at Ross' Hole, however close or distant in reality it actually was to Russell's depiction of it, gave the Corps of Discovery what it needed to continue on, and ultimately succeed, in their journey to the western ocean. It was a vital and critical moment in the expedition, and, as they rested and resupplied there we might use the occasion to reflect on just what sort of men had come to this place we now know as the Bitterroot.

Lewis and Clark together are forever preserved in American history as an amalgamation of leadership that forged the great epic of western exploration of this nation in 1804-1806. Each of these men was a strongly independent individual, but together they melded their talents and genius into a solidarity of command unequalled by any other American explorers. Their friendship was born in shared army experiences for the six months Meriwether Lewis served under Captain William Clark in the Chosen Rifle Company at Fort Greenville, Ohio, in 1796, and was nurtured by the respect each man developed for the other.

Both men were native Virginians although Clark moved to

Captain
William Clark
(Illustration
by Diann Ladd)

Kentucky at age fourteen and grew up on the frontier. Lewis was born into the landed gentry. His mother, Lucy Meriwether, and his father, William Lewis, were both born into distinguished Virginia families and were neighbors of Thomas Jefferson. Clark, the ninth of ten children, also came from a respected military family, and young William followed in the footsteps of his older brother, war hero General George Rogers Clark, who was also a friend of Jefferson.

Captain William Clark retired from the army in 1786 because of ill health and also to care for his brother, George. At the age of eighteen Lewis took over the family farm and became expert at managing, organizing and supervising the farm and the workers. He later volunteered in the militia to put down the Whiskey Rebellion and rose to the rank of captain. As youngsters both men lived on the frontier, where they learned the ways of the wilderness and the skills to survive there. Both families were patriots during the Revolution; both young men admired Thomas Jefferson and his policies.

*Captain
Meriwether Lewis
(Illustration
by Diann Ladd)*

Lewis was the better educated of the two, having attended Latin school from age thirteen to eighteen. During his two years as private secretary to President Jefferson he listened, questioned, studied and explored the ideas and scientific and political thought swirling around the Jefferson Administration in the early years of the nineteenth century, 1801-1803. When the President selected the eager young Lewis to command the Expedition to the West, he also sent him to Philadelphia to be educated and trained by experts in the fields of natural sciences and celestial navigation. Meanwhile, Clark, four years older than Lewis, was himself being educated in the time-honored school of hands-on-experience. He became an excellent frontiersman, woodsman, boatman, Indian fighter, and a natural leader among the rough and rugged frontiersmen he commanded. That he was not formally educated is evident in his journal writing and spelling, of which he was always well aware. He frequently asked Lewis' help in composing letters and often copied Lewis' writing into his own journals.

When Meriwether Lewis accepted the command of the Corps of Discovery in 1802, there was no doubt in his mind about whom he would chose to accompany him and to share the command of the Expedition. Lewis invited Clark to join him as co-commander of the Expedition: *"Thus my friend,…you have a summary view of the plan, the means and the objects of this expedition. If therefore there is anything under those circumstances, in this enterprise, which would induce you to participate with me in it's fatiegues, it's danger and it's honors, believe me there is no man on earth with whom I should feel equal pleasuure in sharing them as with yourself."[1]*

Clark replied, *"This is an undertaking fraited with many dificulties, but My friend I do assure you that no man lives with whome I would perful to undertake Such a Trip &c. as yourself. My friend I join you with hand & Heart."[2]*

Thus from the strength of their knowledge of and respect for each other, these two men, co-partners in command, developed a successful team, the Corps of Discovery, which achieved one of the most amazing voyages of exploration ever undertaken. Like a magnet attaches to metal, a hand fits into a glove, they worked, planned, shared and cared for one another. Each man complimented the other. Where Lewis was shaky, Clark was strong and vice versa. Both young men were tall, athletic, confident, courageous and capable. Each accepted and respected the other's word as his bond. Both were intelligent, natural leaders who shared the work with their men and did not ask more of them than of themselves. Each captain developed a shrewd discernment of character and fitness as they selected the individuals who would make up the Corps of Discovery, but they also treated each individual fairly and with sensitivity. They could and would push their men to the limit but never beyond their capacity.

The noted historian-writer Bernard DeVoto assessed these leaders as follows: Lewis was the diplomat and the commercial thinker; Clark the negotiator. Lewis was the scientific specialist; Clark, the engineer and geographer. Both were experienced boatmen, but Clark had greater skill and was the master of frontier crafts. Both men were highly intelligent as was evident in the meticulous planning and organization of the expedition. Lewis was the natural scientist, Clark, the cartographer, "a genius" claimed Montana historian, K.

Ross Toole. They were masters of every situation and successfully handled every emergency".[3] They never appeased their potential enemies but faced them down, a quality which earned the respect of their followers as well as the Indians they met along the way.

Both Lewis and Clark were products of the society of their births, the slave-holding culture of the South. Although they recognized and respected the Indians they met both as individuals and as nations, they avoided extending the same respect to negroes. Lewis was assured of the superiority of the white race, and, although Clark adopted and educated Sacajawea's and Charbonneau's child, Jean Baptiste, a half-Indian, he refused to give his black servant, York, his freedom after the Corps return. York had carried his weight throughout the journey, was faithful and dependable and deserved recognition. Yet Clark did not free York to join his wife for another ten years.

They differed in personality. Lewis was intense, cool and detached, preferring solitude in hiking alone, observing and writing in his journals to the camaraderie that a gregarious Clark shared with the men. However, both captains instinctively knew, and always retained, their positions of leadership. Lewis did not dislike Indians, but he could never quite share the warm affection Clark had for Sacajawea, whom Clark called "Janey", and for her son, Jean Baptiste, whom he nicknamed "Pomp." Lewis was a brilliant leader, but he had a short temper and suffered from melancholy, a trait inherited from his father's family. Today his condition might be diagnosed as "bi-polar or manic-depressive." Still, to his credit, Lewis's strong self-discipline and the importance he attached to this mission in fulfilling his dream of adventure enabled him to temper his moods and to avoid sliding too far into depression. Clark's personality, more sanguine than Lewis', was more constant and thereby served to compliment the party's leadership needs.

Did the captains make mistakes? Yes, they did. They were human, but as Bernard De Voto put it, "They were adept at contriving expedients."[4] Some mistakes were small and non-consequential; others they corrected, such as Captain Clark's decision on the return trip eastward. Rather than return by the same arduous route that the Corps had taken in September of 1805 on their journey over the Bitterroots, from the Shoshone village to Ross' Hole, Captain Clark chose the path favored by the Ootlashoots, the Salish, and crossed over the Continental Divide to the Big Hole Basin via a pass that later came to be known as Gibbons Pass. There were also big mistakes, i.e. Captain Lewis' exploration of the Marias and close encounter with the Blackfeet in which the party escaped capture and probably death by combinations of quick thinking, quicker action, and sheer luck. Another mistake which they paid for was the decision not to heed the advice of the Nez Perce Indians, who counseled them to wait for the snow to melt on the Bitterroot Mountains before attempting their return passage in the spring of 1806. The Corps was forced back on the only retrograde march of the whole journey.

The men they chose were a rough and rugged lot, who had to be disciplined, even to the point of being flogged, court-martialed, and dismissed. But after six months of intensive training under the two captains, the members of the Corps of Discovery were in good

This statue commemorating the Lewis and Clark Expedition, by sculptor Robert Scriver, is in Great Falls, Montana. Depicted in it are Captains Meriwether Lewis and William Clark, as well as Clark's slave, York, and Lewis' Newfoundland Retriever, Seaman. (Photo by Dale A. Burk)

physical shape, alert, dependable and eager to begin the great adventure. They were now a sound military unit, one which would earn the respect of their leaders. How did the men appraise their captains? On June 9, 1805, the Expedition was at the fork of the Missouri and the Marias River in what is now northern Montana. The two captains studied their maps, discussed the situation and were convinced and in agreement that they should follow the south fork. The men, however, to a man, were convinced otherwise. "Take the north fork," they advised. The captains would not change their minds. In a remarkable tribute to their leaders, the men accepted their decision and followed the south fork cheerfully and without a note of dissension. Fortunately, the captains were right. The south fork was the Missouri River.

After he was no longer under the captain' command, Joseph Whitehouse wrote of *"the manly and soldier-like behavior and enterprizing abilities, of both Captain Lewis and Captain Clark...and the humanity shown at all times by them, to those under their command on this perilous and important voyage of discovery."*[5]

The Men of the Corps of Discovery

It is difficult to think of the famous expedition as a military unit, but that is exactly what it was — an aspect of the journey that has been forgotten with the passing years and remarkable accomplishments made by such a small group of individuals. By the time the Expedition had reached the Bitterroot valley the men had formed a hardened core of friendship driven by a common goal and forged in the fires of danger and seemingly insurmountable hardships. A deep respect for the integrity and leadership of Lewis and Clark was also paramount to the deep camaraderie pervading this unit.

The military roster was comprised of Captains Meriwether Lewis and William Clark, four sergeants and twenty-five privates. Other essential members were Clark's slave, York, two interpreters, Drouillard and Charbonneau, his wife, Sacajawea, their young son Jean Baptiste Charbonneau — plus Lewis' black Newfoundland dog, Seaman.

Complete success was possible by virtue of the skill and courage displayed by the individuals chosen for this awesome endeavor. They were hunters, rivermen, blacksmiths, carpenters, cooks, tailors, as well as interpreters and trackers. Each man had to wear many hats and along with expertise, a lot of plain old back-breaking physical labor was required to navigate upriver against the current and carry heavy loads at the many portages. The wilderness had been a classroom of sorts. By the time the men reached the Bitterroot Valley, they were adept at new skills which necessity demanded.

There were the three sergeants, John Ordway, Nathaniel Pryor and Patrick Gass, who were responsible for organizing the daily routine and logistics of the Expedition. Well educated Ordway kept a journal, as well as meticulous books. Patrick Gass, of Irish descent, became a sergeant upon the death of Charles Floyd early in the journey, apparently of appendicitis, just above the mouth of the

Looking south from the upper end of Camp Creek, this is the route from which the Expedition came into the Bitterroot, picking its way off the high ridge in the center background and down into the draw to reach the Bitterroot headwaters stream course that ultimately became known as Camp Creek. This scene was both snow-covered and hidden in clouds and fog when the Expedition came this way in September of 1805 on its arduous crossing into the Bitterroot. (Photo by Pat Hastings)

Platte River on August 20, 1804. Sergeant Gass excelled in carpentry and boat building.

The roster of privates and the talents they brought to the Expedition is varied. William Bratton, of Irish descent, was a superior gunsmith, blacksmith and hunter and also proved useful in salt making. Besides being a hunter, John Collins, was also one of the cooks, even using that talent to make beer from Camas roots. John Colter was a fine hunter and invaluable in reconnoitering. Pierre Cruzatte, half French and half Omaha Indian, was nicknamed "St. Peter" by the party and was chosen for his river knowledge but his many other talents in sign talk, translating and hunting, made him an important member of the party. He would play a vital part in negotiations with the Oot-la-shoots (Salish) at Ross' Hole, but it was

The Expedition's first camp in the Bitterroot, and the point at which they met the Salish, is at the nothern end of the Camp Creek drainage where it ties into Ross' Hole in the background of this photo. They encamped a hundred yards or so off the end of the ridge at the left of the photo and the Salish encampment was just beyond in Ross' Hole. Undoubtedly the scene in the bottom of both the Camp Creek drainage and Ross' Hole was greatly different in 1805. (Photo by Pat Hastings)

his fiddle playing night after night in the camp that probably did much to restore the morale of the men as they danced and sang off the trials of the day.

Joseph and Reuben Field were brothers and excellent woodsmen and hunters. Joseph took charge of the salt making while at Fort Clatsop and also displayed his versatility by handcrafting two seats and a writing table for the officer's hut. His brother, Reuben, was known as one of the fastest runners in the party. Robert Frazier, from Vermont, showed an interest in learning the Nez Perce language; he made such an impression with the Nez Perce that they made him a gift of one of their horses. The fisherman of the party, Silas Goodrich, provided a welcome change of fare for the men. George Gibson, a fine hunter and horseman, joined in with his own violin during those evenings around the campfire. Hugh Hall seemed only to have distinguished himself as one who liked his drink and was also one of the more adventurous of the party. Captain Clark said of Thomas Howard that he never drank water. Howard was recruited from an infantry company.

Francis Labiche, exceptional in many areas, was half French and half Omaha Indian. He was adept in French, English and several Indian languages, which made him an invaluable interpreter. Labiche was a patron of one of the piroques, a dugout boat similar to a canoe. He was a competent waterman, tracker and hunter, often providing waterfowl for the evening's menu. Hugh McNeal was recruited from the infantry and was a faithful member of the corps. John Shields, the oldest member of the party, was an outstanding hunter and woodsman. Private Shields was the head blacksmith, gunsmith, boat builder and general repair man. During the winter and spring of 1804-05 while the party camped with the Mandan Indians it was Shield's blacksmith work, used as a trading commodity with the Indians, that kept the men of the Expedition in corn and other foodstuffs. He seemed to be versatile in many areas, being the one to suggest that William Bratton take sweathouse treatments for his back pain. It must be said that he contributed much to the success of the venture. George Shannon, the youngest man in the party, was another of the capable hunters providing a good portion of the game. He was also noted as a good singer.

John Potts, from Dillenburg, Germany, had been a miller before being recruited. John Baptiste Lapage enlisted at Fort

Mandan. John Thompson, William Werner and Peter Weiser all served as cooks for the Expedition. Weiser also often served as quartermaster as well. Richard Windsor, a useful member of the Corps was often listed with the hunting parties. Alexander Willard was not only a fine blacksmith and gunsmith but also a good hunter. Joseph Whitehouse, the party's principal "hidecurer" and tailor, made and repaired much of the men's clothes on the expedition.

The two civilian interpreters hired were George Drouillard and Toussaint Charbonneau. Drouillard, half Shawnee Indian, possessed a wide array of talents. He was an ace hunter and scout, and one of the best woodsman and trackers in the party. He was also a capable diplomat and "spoke" fluent Indian sign language. Drouillard was unique in that Captains Lewis and Clark even involved him in matters of expedition strategy. Charbonneau's largest contribution appears to be his child bride, Sacajawea and her young son, Jean Baptiste, nicknamed "Pomp" by Captain Clark.

Last, but certainly not least, there was Captain Clark's slave, York. (Could it really be that he was just York?) For having been born a slave he had no legal rights, even the right of ownership. It seems that a last name was not given to him for we know him only as York. He apparently did more than his share of the work. But to those Indians who had never seen a black man he was considered "Big Medicine." His remarkable physical appearance was viewed with awe and astonishment by the Indians and he provided an entry for the white strangers that might not otherwise have been possible. What must York have thought, as the Indians honored him because of his size and rich color, the very color that had sentenced him to life as a slave? We can only wonder. Whatever, he was an invaluable member of the party.

The success of this endeavor was made possible through the teamwork of these individuals. Each man put aside his own concerns and had only an eye for the needs of the military unit. The struggles which they encountered only deepened their resolve. It is interesting to read Captain Lewis' closing comments to the Secretary of War, Henry Dearborn, upon his presentation of the roster of men who served on the expedition. On January 15, 1807. He wrote:

"With respect to all those persons whose names are entered on this roll, I feel a peculiar pleasure in declaring, that the ample support which they gave me under every difficulty; the manly firmness

which they evinced on every necessary occasion; and the patience and fortitude with which they submitted to, and bore, the fatigues and painful sufferings incident to my late tour to the Pacific Ocean, entitles them to my warmest approbbation and thanks; nor will I suppress the expression of a hope, that the recollection of services thus faithfully performed will meet a just reward in an ample remuneration on the part of our Government. "[6]

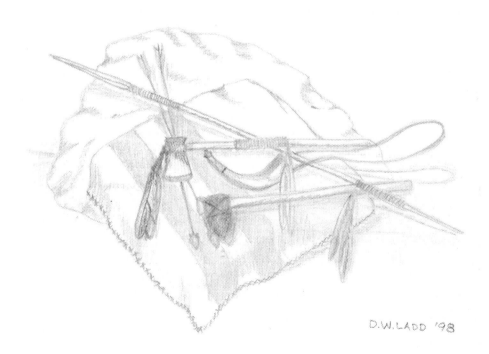

D.W.LADD '98

CHAPTER FOUR

MEETING THE SALISH

ROSS' HOLE IS in a wide valley in western Montana where Camp Creek flows into the East Fork of the Bitterroot River. It is eighteen miles south of Darby, Montana, near Sula on U.S. Highway 93 and is a broad plain threaded by a beautiful, willow-lined stream and flanked by steep, stately mountains.

On March 12, 1824, Alexander Ross, a fur trader employed by the Hudson Bay Company, was leading a party of fifty-five Indian and white trappers, eighty-nine women and children and 392 horses toward the pass into the Big Hole when deep snow stranded them. For nearly a month the party struggled desperately to break through the drifts and cross to the Big Hole before they finally made it, April 15, 1824. Although Ross' Hole is named for him, Alexander Ross referred to it as "The Valley of Troubles" for the hardships and struggles endured there.

There, the Corps of Discovery met the Oot-la-shoots, a band of Indians belonging to the Tushepa Tribe, the Salish (sometimes referred to as "Flathead," a misnomer). How astonished these Indians must have been to see this strange party of men and one Indian woman with a baby traveling through their homeland. A Salish tradition, recorded ninety years later, states that Chief Three Eagles was out scouting for enemies who might be prowling around waiting to steal their horses. When he sighted Lewis and Clark riding horses and a number of men following and leading their horses, Chief Three Eagles was amazed and puzzled. These strangers wore no blankets. Could their blankets have been stolen? The men were pale, worn and haggard, and did not look like a war party. Still one of the men was

"Lewis and Clark Meeting The Indians at Ross' Hole," oil by Charles M. Russell, 1912. Courtesy Montana Historical Society.

Charles M. Russell's Painting
"Lewis And Clark Meeting The Indians at Ross' Hole"

"Lewis and Clark Meeting The Indians at Ross' Hole" is a visual story, the masterpiece of western artist Charles M. Russell and perhaps the most famous artistic work ever involving a Montana setting. In this painting Russell immortalized the historical moment when the Corps of Discovery, after a grueling trip through and over the Bitterroot Mountains from the Lemhi into the Bitterroot, discover the camp of the Oot-la-shoot Indians, (the Flatheads or Salish), September 4, 1805, as the tribe was preparing to leave on its annual buffalo hunt east of the mountains. This meeting was critical to the Corps of Discovery as the Indians held the key to the continuance and success of the Expedition, primarily through the horses they provided in trade. Indian horses and riders dominate the center foreground in the painting, and bring sweeping action and breadth to the scene of this historic encounter. At the right the two captains wait patiently and cautiously as their Shoshone guide, the main figure, which is drawn with dramatic intensity, is conversing and translating with the Oot-la-shoots. On the sidelines Sacajawea squats with her baby on her back as York, holding a musket in his arms, attends the horses and watches attentively behind his master, Captain Clark. In the background those formidable mountains are somewhat obscured by clouds, but Trapper's Peak is recognizable in the left upper corner.

Writer Patricia Burnham noted in an article about the painting in Montana History, The Magazine of the Montana Historical Society, *that "One of the principal tenets of traditional history painting held that the artist's most necessary and noble function was to instruct the viewer."[1] Here Russell certainly imparts his lesson, the conscious narrative of the Indian before the Americans' arrival. Charles M. Russell was fascinated by the exploits of Lewis and Clark, and Burnham makes a key point about Russell's artistic intent in her article about the painting: "He (Russell) lavished dramatic treatment on the people who would soon be vanquished, knowing full well the unfathomable power that lay behind the gentle intruders."[2]*

The painting has been called one of the truly great pictures of America. It was commissioned by the State of Montana and completed by Russell on July 12, 1912. The mural measures 12 feet by 25 feet; it hangs behind the speaker's platform in the chamber of the House of Representatives at the Montana State Capitol in Helena.

painted black, the sign of a warrior, but an Indian woman and baby rode with them. Warriors did not bring women and children on a war party. Assured in his mind that these men were not looking for trouble, Chief Three Eagles returned to the Salish camp and described what he had seen.

At this point the Indians could have assaulted the white men, stolen their goods, especially their guns and horses, and destroyed the Expedition. They did not. And although the Salish were anxious to be on their way to join their allies to hunt buffalo, they were also curious about these travelers and the black man with them. Consequently, they welcomed the strangers. The chiefs covered the shoulders of the two captains with white fur robes, their sign of friendship. *"The Chiefs harangued until late at night. Smoked our pipe and appeared satisfied. I was the first white man who ever wer on the waters of this river"[1]* Captain Clark wrote in his journal.

Charles Russell immortalized this meeting in a monumental painting of Lewis and Clark meeting the Flathead Indians at Ross Hole. This painting was commissioned by the state of Montana in 1911. It is considered by many to be Russell's masterpiece and has been called one of the truly great pictures of America. It now hangs in the House of Representatives in the Montana state capitol in Helena.

From Clark's journal, September 04, 1805: *"those Indians well-dressed with skin shirt and robes, they Stout and light complected more So than common for Indians.[2]*

In his journal, September 5, 1805, Joseph Whitehouse described the Salish *"as the liklyest and honest Savages we have ever yet seen. They behave very kind to our party, and are very honest, not attempting to pilfer the most trifling article from us"[3]*

Olin D. Wheeler describes the Salish as, *"No tribe of Indians in the United States has received more and higher encomiums than have these Oot-la-shoots, Salish, or Flatheads, whose knowledge of white and black men was first obtained through Lewis and Clark. Their standards of honesty and morality were and are higher than those of most Indians."[4]*

Clark estimated the Indians number as about 33 lodges, 400 people and 500 horses. The captains decided to encamp at this place

Kinnikinnick
September 4, 1805

D.W. LADD '98

to the right of the Indian lodges. Like the Shoshone, the Salish had only dried berries and roots to eat — no meat, but they shared what they had with the strangers. However, they were well-dressed in sheep skins and buffalo robes. Their horses were the pride and the wealth of these Indians, who kept them in prime condition. The Bitterroot Valley offered excellent pasture for their ponies which were valued by the tribe not only as pack animals but also as racehorses. When the friendly tribes gathered together for dancing and games, they also raced their horses against one another.

In the 1880's and 90's, Marcus Daly, an Irish immigrant, who made a fortune mining copper in Butte, recognized the Bitterroot valley as a prime location for training race horses. He then indulged his Irish born love of horses and horse racing by establishing a stable and building a track near Hamilton. His horses proved Mr. Daly's hunches were right, and they brought back trophies and prize money to their owner. By the end of the century the Daly stable was known and respected in the eastern racing circuit. When Mr. Daly died in 1901, the horses were sold and the stable colors, copper and gold were brought down. However, Marcus Daly's granddaughter, Countess Margit Bessenyey, inherited her grandfather's love of horses. When the Nazis invaded Hungary the Countess offered protection to the famous Lippizaner stallions, which were rescued from Austria during the Nazi occupation at the time of World War II. She then established the Bitterroot Stock Farm, from where she bred and sold her registered horses. After her sudden death in 1987 the horses were sold and dispersed.[5]

While the Indians cherished their horses, their dogs did not fare so well. Both John Ordway and Patrick Gass noted in their journals that the dogs were ravenous — *"eat part of our moccasins"* — *four or five pair. "*[6]

The Expedition was now at a critical point in the journey. The horses obtained from the Shoshone were weak, worn, and crippled. Without fresh horses the Expedition could not survive the hazardous and possibly insurmountable Bitterroot mountains which blocked their way to the Pacific Ocean. The Salish Indians now held the key to the Expedition's survival and success — **horses.** On September 5, 1805, the drama began. The American flag was hoisted, the translators were brought up and the council began. The Salish language proved quite different from the Shoshone which Sacajawea understood. Fortunately, a Shoshone lad lived among the Salish and was able to translate Salish into Shoshone for Sacajawea, who passed the message on to her husband, Charbonneau, in the Hidatsa language.

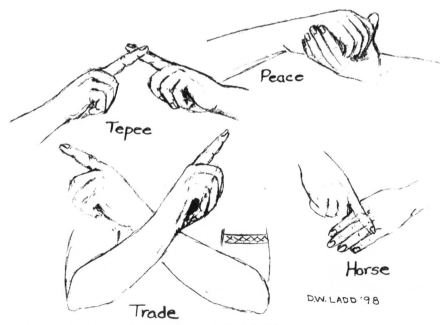

Peace

Tepee

Trade

Horse

D.W. LADD '98

Some elements of the sign language of the times.

Charbonneau then translated to Labiche in French who delivered the message to the captains in English. Along the way, Droulliard was probably there to help in sign language if necessary. The translation then reversed from the English of the captains down the chain to the Salish. In "Hi-Lites of the Bitterroot," July 4, 1997, Dr. Gene Swanzey observes "Horse trading is not much different from buying a used car. Can one adequately imagine buying a used car through five translations up and five back down?" Somehow it worked for the Americans and for the Salish, and Lewis and Clark got the horses they needed.

What trade goods did the Expedition bring with them? Blue beads were the most preferred, and were valued as silver and gold. Knives, scissors, strips of metal, vermillion from the Orient, little mirrors, silver bells, thimbles, gold and silver bands, arrowheads, ribbons, rings, earrings, and fish hooks were some of the trade goods favored by the natives. The chiefs received special peace medals and flags. Note that the flags had fifteen stars and fifteen stripes at that time. — From "The Traveling Trunk: a presentation made by George Knapp and Chuck Sundstrom, members of the Traveller's Rest Chapter of the Lewis and Clark National Heritage Foundation.

According to Whitehouse the captains assured the Indians that *"we came to make peace between all red people who were at Warr with each other and to instruct them in the way of Trade, and that they would open the Path from their nation to the white people."*[7][4]

Because the Salish were anxious to obtain arms to defend themselves against their enemies, and because they were a friendly and generous people and did not recognize the desperate situation of the Expedition, the captains were able to obtain twelve strong horses, including two mares with colts, swapped seven lame ones and bought ten saddles all for a small amount of merchandise; four medals to the chiefs, some shirts, flags and tobacco. What a moment of relief for the captains and their followers! Had the Salish realized how much the Expedition depended on their horses, would the captains have been able to trade so well? And, would it be correct to surmise that without the Salish horses the Expedition would have perished? It very well could have.

On The Meeting With the Salish

President Jefferson's planning and outfitting of the Voyage of Discovery's journey from St. Louis to the Pacific Ocean and back brought a lengthy letter of instruction to Captain Lewis on 20th June, 1803. Among the instructions and mandates given by Jefferson was a comprehensive list of categories for Capt. Lewis to note and record as the Expedition met and assembled with the Indians along the course of discovery — and they were applied directly to the Expedition's encounter with the Indians at Ross' Hole in the Bitterroot. This charge followed:

"The commerce which may be carried on with the people inhabiting the line you will pursue renders a knowlege [knowledge] of these people important. You will therefore endeavor to make yourself acquainted, as far as a diligent pursuit of your journey shall admit with the names of the nations and their numbers.... In all your intercourse with the Indians, treat them in the most friendly and conciliatory manner which their own conduct will admit...make them acquainted with the character and commercial disposition of the U. S. , and of our wish to be neighborly, friendly, and useful to them, and our disposition to a commercial intercourse with them."[8]

The Expedition was headed into uncharted, alien territory and Jefferson felt some anxiety. He was apprehensive about the unknowable danger facing the men and reactions to it.

"It is impossible to forsee in what manner you will be received by those people"...and "the degree of perseverance with which you are to pursue your journey ... to your discretion therefore must be left the degree of danger you may risk ... we wish you to err on the side of safety and bring back your party safe ... even if it be with less information ... we value too much the lives of citizens to offer them to probable destruction."[9]

Heeding Jefferson's caution, and also not wanting to be thought an easy mark for aggressive activity, Lewis took precaution to discourage raids or skirmishes. A well regulated camp was maintained with guards trained for confrontation and ready to relay signals of alert in the camp. Lewis had great discipline and expected the same of his men. He required daily inspection of rifles and other fighting equipment, knowing preparedness was the best defense against continuous and aggressive behaviors.[10]

On the evening of September 4, 1805, the Corps of Discovery came into a large, lovely grassy valley now known as Ross' Hole. The Indians they encountered there introduced themselves as the Oot-la-shoots of the Tushepau nation.

Who, exactly, were these people? The Oot-la-shoots were Salish speaking, part of the language family who for the most part came from, or lived along, the Columbia River system and its plateaus. They were called Flatheads by other tribes and traders. The origin of the name Flathead is uncertain. As a result there are many theories about it, since the Oot-la-shoots did not practice head-shaping as did their language relatives along the coast. An account by Adolf Hungry Wolf theorizes, a friendly band from the coast who did practice head shaping was visiting the Oot-la-shoots; the visitors were seen by outsiders, and believed to live in the Bitterroot, which led people to call the Oot-la-shoots, Flatheads. Some believe the name was perpetuated by Lewis and Clark who misnamed them and the misinformation was subsequently disseminated through their journals and papers. Adding to the confusion, the sign language gesture which named the Oot-la-shoots was made by pressing hands on both sides of the head (or one in front the other back) indicating an attempt to flatten or shape the head. Intertribal sign language was used extensively by Indians, and some traders, for barter and trade, and also for conversing across dialect and language barriers. The gestured names given to tribes signified a special attribute, ornament, or individuality of the tribe. Some believe the widespread use of sign language among tribes and traders locked the Flathead name in place.

"Our guide could not speake the language of these people but soon engaged them in conversation by signs or jesticulation, the common language of all the [Indians] of North America, it is one understood by all of them and appears to be sufficiently copious to convey with a degree of certainty the outlines of what they wish to communicate."[11] — Capt. Lewis, September 10, 1805

There was no mention of the Oot-la-shoots having flattened heads when they met the Expedition. They were described by

Sergeant Whitehouse and others as a handsome and well made people. Present-day Flatheads prefer to be called Salish, a term which better suits them.

Expedition members were fascinated by the sound of the Salish language. Sergeant Whitehouse and Captain Clark said it had a throaty, *"gurgling"* tone spoken as with a *"burr on the tongue," "they appear to us to have an Empediment in their Speech or a brough...."* Sergeant Ordway said simply, *"these natives have the Stranges language of any we have ever yet seen...we think perhaps that they are the welch Indians, & C."*[12]

Bernard DeVoto calls the Welsh Indians the "most durable myth in American history." It first appeared in 1583. Now, over two hundred years later, the men were full of speculation concerning it. The tribe was thought to have descended from a Twelfth Century Welsh prince and his followers who colonized part of America, and were now somewhere in the western wilderness.

President Jefferson was among the noteworthies interested in verifying the tribe's reality. He alerted Capt. Lewis to be observant, and Lewis, following that mandate, took time to capture the Salish vocabulary, as he had done with other tribes. This time, however, it was for comparison with the Welsh language. We don't know if the analysis was completed when they returned, but modern scholars could find no similarity between the Salish language and the Welsh. The Bitterroot Valley did not house the so-called Welsh Indians.

The Bitterroot Salish lived in skin lodges and dressed in plains style skin clothing. The women wore an A-line skin dress which was long, extending to the ankles and made of two full skins. It retained the basic shape of the hide. The sewing which connected the front and back hides was done from the waist to the bottom. The seam from under arm to waist was open, which was utilitarian as this enabled the woman to swivel the dress slightly for ease in nursing her baby, and also provided a wide range of arm movement which was beneficial for her daily work.

A belt was worn, which was most often decorated, and fastened with thongs strung through holes in the ends of the belt. There were two tails or appendages on the belt which hung directly down the front of the dress.

The skirt might be decorated with fringe at the bottom. Shells, beads, or fringe strung on thongs hung from the bottom of the yoke which would be embroidered, as might the sleeve bands.

Women wore simple accessories. Necklaces of sea snails or elk teeth might be worn. When beads were unavailable, strings of cream colored, thinly cut, hollow bones were strung and worn. Sometimes many strands of varying lengths were worn depending on the wealth of the family or the occasion.

Low moccasins were used in warm weather. They were one-seamed, and not highly decorated. In the winter a wrapping or leg piece was attached to the moccasin. Dress moccasins usually had a decorated leg wrapping. Both the dress and winter wrapping laced on the leg above the moccasin.

The Salish man's life revolved around war and hunting, consequently clothing for him was functional and dependent on the type of activity he was engaged in, the season, or individual fancy. The breech cloth was most often worn. It was made of a rectangle of skin strung from a thong around the waist. A skin shirt was worn over it which extended to the knees or mid-thigh. The sleeves were stitched together and the sides were laced with thongs. The shirt was usually decorated with fringe. A leather belt was worn, depending on the occasion or activity. Men's belts were wider than those of women and did not have long tails, but were more decorated. Blue was the favorite color for the margin band that surrounded the panel of design on the belt.

Leggings were worn in the winter, and for ceremonial occasions, and times when they would not handicap action or performance. They were made of a tapered piece of skin reaching from ankle to hip and were fastened by strings to a leather belt around the waist. The bottom near the ankle was laced for a tighter fit. They were usually decorated, most often with leather fringe.

Men's moccasins often had a second sole attached which afforded cushioning against stones and prickles, and muffled their movement when hunting or stalking enemy camps. Some of their moccasins were highly decorated. They were one-seamed, made of elk or deer dressed skin. Extensions or trailers were sewn into the seam at the base of the heel for decorative effect. Trailers were often small animal tails or fringes.

In winter, robes, mittens and hats were added. Robes were made from buffalo, elk, deer, bear, sheep, and other animal skins. The hair was worn or used inside, close to the body. Skin mittens and fur caps were used, as well as moccasins with the hair left on the skin and turned inside.

Decoration for clothing in earlier days was primarily quill embroidery in various naturally dyed colors; red from berries and roots, yellow from pine tree lichen, blue from duck manure, green from grasses. Quill embroidery was usually designed geometrically. After white trade developed in the area, embroidery with beads became more prevalent. Later, the missionaries recognized the Salish women's natural gift for design and stimulated them to make patterns other than geometric ones. Much of the floral design began during that period. Most animal or commemorative designs were for men who admired and wanted qualities like those of animals depicted.

Other decorative items for clothing and wear were; plain leather fringe either single or double layered; lengths of shells and trade beads strung on thongs; fringe made of numerous weasel or wild ermine tails; metal or brass thimbles, bells, nailheads, shells exchanged in barter with Pacific Coast Indians; seeds, claws, bones, buttons, feathers, paint, braided sweet grass, and more. Eagle feathers were highly prized. The eagle represented power and strength and the Creation of the Great Spirit. Its spirit is believed to be alive in even the smallest feather. The feathers are used in celebrations, battles, and for Indian medicine.

Earrings, if worn, were most often iridescent clam shells, tied on a thong of soft leather and placed over the ear. Necklaces and bracelets varied with wealth and the whim of the individual. Men wore more decorative items then women. Men used color on their skin for ceremonies and specific occasions. The color was obtained from various clays which were mixed with fats or oils for application. The red, yellow, purple, and white clay was powder like and carried in pouches. Charcoal was used for black decoration.

Buckskin clothing was cleaned with pipe-clay, which was found in abundance in some parts of the country and traded. The women stored clothing with wild herbs to infuse them with fresh fragrance. The clothing was made by women, and each family member had at least two or three changes. There were no needles. Sewing was accomplished with the use of a pointed bone from the foreleg of a deer, for which a wooden handle was made to enable a better grip. The bone awl was used to pierce the leather, after which strips of sinew were slipped through the holes. Sinew from the long tendons of the deer's neck was used. It is first dried, then separated into strips which need moisture to become pliant. Women carried the sinew and awl, and perhaps other 'tools,' in buckskin bags.

"...we met a party of the Flathead, Tushepau nation of 33 Lodges, about 80 men 400 Total and at least 500 horses,...."[13] — *Capt. Clark, Sept. 4, 1805*

There were more women than men at the Salish camp. The attrition of war, raids and hunting accidents was great, male infant death and the inclusion of captured women in the victor's camp, or sold to other tribes, could be additional factors. Polygamy helped the situation. If they were able, Salish men could take more than one wife. Often the wife's younger sister was incorporated into their household. If a young married man was killed, one of his brothers was expected to marry his widow. She could marry someone else, however, given the permission of her in-laws. Protecting women in these matters helped maintain tribal strength and cohesion, as the women were afforded physical protection and provided with shelter, clothing and food. The husband, as warrior, was a physical safeguard and from hunts provided meat, skins, and materials. She, among other things, made clothing, meals, and household articles from his provisions.

As with modern woman, the Indian woman's work seemed endless. The man's work was often dangerous, strenuous, and frequently fatal. Women dressed all the skins, gathered and cured the berries and roots, which often carried them through long winters and other thin times, she erected and maintained the lodge and its equipment, gathered firewood and water, prepared most meals, made most of the clothing, dried, butchered, and processed the meat, had complete care of the children until their education began, which was determined by gender, and other duties. Men hunted, fought, made specific clothing, most tools and all weapons, and maintained the horses.

Captain Clark noted that women who labored to provide food were more respected by men. Plains women, whose role was believed secondary to men in securing means of survival for the camp, were not as esteemed as Northwest women who gathered roots and berries to supplement their diet and sometimes fished.

The Salish wife owned everything except weapons and horses, which were the husband's possessions. She could do as she chose with the lodge and all its articles, the clothing and food.

Girls were marriageable after puberty. Boys married after establishing themselves as hunters and warriors. When a Salish man did a particularly honorable deed of bravery, usually against an enemy, he was allowed to count coup, or count the deed as an honor and notch his coup stick. A notched coup stick meant that a young man could claim a bride without consulting her parents. By tapping her on the shoulder with his coup stick he indicated his intentions, and if she did not move it off, it meant she had given her consent to the match. Within the Scalp dance, which was performed by women in men's clothing, there was a particular section of the dance in which if a woman chose to place her rod over the shoulder of a man and he did not push it away, they were considered married.

Babies slept in buffalo hide bags. When not in them or wiggling and exercising legs and arms on robes and skins, they were for most of the day in cradleboards with a filling of moss or skunk cabbage which served as diapers. Young girls in the family would look after the baby while it was awake. They also helped gather firewood, hauled water and performed other chores. Younger boys and girls spent much of their time outside in play. Play was mostly games of skill in preparation for adult life. Many kinds of toys were made for children; small bows and arrows and horses, dolls with clothing and miniature cradle boards. Play acting, acting incorporating mythological characters and mimicry of animals were favorite activities. In addition, a game called cat's-cradle which used many figures of birds, animals and people, was used considerably to engage children.

Boys practiced hunting. They learned to snare birds like grouse and prairie chickens in loop snares made of sinew thread. They also set snares over gopher and woodchuck holes. The captured birds were taken home to be roasted near an open fire, or boiled in a robe lined pit or in a woven airtight container to which hot stones were added until the water boiled and the meat was done. The broth and meat were eaten with various roots, like wild onion, carrot or celery, camas, bitterroot, and/or bread cakes made from wild berries like chokecherries, serviceberries, plums and huckleberries.

Much of the fishing done by young boys was in the winter.

Chokecherry

D.W. LADD '98

Fishing line was made of woven hair from horses's tail. A piece of thorn bush was cut to serve as a hook, the stem being attached to the woven hair line with sinew. The catch was taken home for meal preparation.

Chiefs did not exercise authority binding on the individuals of the tribe except during crises. They used their character and moral standing as levers of persuasion. The core of the tribe was the family unit, and the family's allegiance to the tribe was seen as binding. The principal, or highest ranking chief of the tribe was an hereditary position. For example, there was a direct genetic line from Chief Three Eagles to Chief Charlot.

A council, consisting of elders and proven younger men of ability met to select the successor of a deceased chief. By custom their choice was limited to the men of the family; as a rule the eldest son was chosen. There might be some discussion of others, but in the usual method of Indian council they reached a common understanding. The minority would say nothing to oppose the general decision. It was expected of the chief that he preserve the peace among the tribal members, select campsites, and decide when they should move elsewhere. He also summoned elders and subchiefs for important matters concerning the tribe.

Because of constant wars, the tribe chose a war chief. This position was not hereditary but chosen yearly. He had no authority at home and was like any other tribal member. But, on hunting excursions within foreign enemy territory, he had almost total authority. He rode lead on the advance and brought up the rear on the return. He had two or three subchiefs for counsel and advice. If any of the tribe fell out of line or committed any other breach of discipline, they received instant reprimand. As these reprimands were committed for the safety of all, the members complained little if at all, the sense of tribal duty overriding resentfulness and indignation. On returning to their Valley the war chief's authority ceased, and the peace chief resumed leadership.

Examples of ponderosa pine from which the Salish stripped the cambium layer for use as food. While these two trees are in the vicinity of the Ross' Hole encampment, it is likely that this pair of trees were stripped many years after the Corps of Discovery was in the area. Many trees with these sort of scars can be found along the Corps' route in the forested parts of the Bitterroot.

Indian Trees

Peeling away the outer tree bark on the Yellow Pine or Ponderosa tree to reach and eat the sap-sweet cambium layer beneath was a Spring activity of which we can still see evidence of the practice in the Bitterroot and elsewhere today. After the women peeled the bark, the cambium was cut into strips six to seven feet long, rolled into balls and stored in green leaves to keep them moist, or tied into knots to be eaten more easily. Cambium was a nutritious as well as delicious food source. It served other functions as well; women processed it and used it for basketry, it was used as an emergency food for horses during snowstorms when grass was unobtainable, or during fast travel when there was limited time for grazing. It was dried and shredded for that purpose.

The Indian trees (or Culturally Scarred Trees as they are now called) are in small groves around the valley and estimated to be between one hundred to three hundred years old, meaning that some of those we see were alive at the time the Expedition passed through the Bitterroot.

The cut or scar on the tree always began two to three feet from the base of the tree, extending six to seven feet in length, and two to three feet wide. The top of the scar was generally rounded or arched. Distinctive flint or axe cuts are visible inside the shallow cavity. Some scars have unique configurations around the wound or scar as the outer bark sealed and the tree's growth continued. A wide scar means the tree was used over a long period of time. Ponderosa pines were peeled in the Bitterroot Valley, Lodgepole pine was used at higher elevations. The Salish chewed the pitchy secretion found on the bark much as we do gum today. They also harvested the seeds for food.

The trees are indicators of travel corridors, meeting places, and resting stops of the valley's Indians.

"Particularly on this Creek the Indians have peeled a number of Pine for the underneath bark which they eate at certain seasons of the year. I am told in Spring they make use of this bark. "[14] — *Capt. Clark, September 12, 1805*

Camping in The Bitterroot

The Bitterroot Valley was a long and lovely valley of nearly one hundred miles, which provided the Salish with many good campsites. Some of the natural features were snow fed creeks, dense evergreen growth along the mountain slopes, hollows and benches, willow thickets and cottonwood groves, a clear winding river, and shady canyons. All terrain factors were considered when choosing a site. Campsites required area which, if necessary, could be defended; it needed a clean water supply for both horses and themselves; plenty of available fuel for cooking and comfortability; and good grazing for horses, which didn't have to be luxuriant, they liked grazing the thinly covered hill grasses.

Residents in the area continue to turn up Indian artifacts in their gardens, fields, and along the roadside. There are pictographs on the walls of valley canyons and ledges. The present town of Victor was named Sweathouse because of the Indian sweat lodges built along the creek banks. Stevensville was a favorite winter campsite and dance ground. The list could go on...

The Sweat lodges in Victor were probably made of willow saplings which grew abundantly along the creeks and river bed. The willow-domed structure was covered with any material which did not allow steam to escape. Inside, water was poured over heated rocks, raising a steaming temperature to unbearable levels. The sweat was generally followed by a cold plunge into the nearby creek.

The Salish used the sweat ritual both ceremonially and medicinally. For both of these it was used to cleanse the body and the mind. Sweat ceremonies were held before major events and challenges. They were used as an aid in preparation for war, hunts, to induce visions, when faced with dangerous or important events, or to ease consequences of mistaken judgment. Medicinally they were used to restore harmony and vitality. Sweats were used for almost all diseases, inflammations and pains. It was sometimes a social activity to take a sweat with friends, and it was a great offense to decline accompanying them if invited.

Sweats are still used today. The survival of the sweathouse, a sacred place of prayer and purification, means the survival of a tribal spiritual tradition.

Excellent Horsemen

The Oot-la-shoots were fine horsemen, as were the women. They participated in activities and games used as opportunities to show their skill as horsemen and athletes, charging, circling, swooping and shouting.

The Indian horse was a fine teachable animal. He was not a beautiful animal, but was sturdy, long winded and tough, possessing great power of endurance. They were used for travel, hunting, especially for buffalo, war, racing, and as pack animals. They were common stakes in gambling, and important articles for trade in intertribal markets and elsewhere. Sergeant Patrick Gass described the Oot-la-shoots this way in his journal:

"They are a friendly people; have plenty of robes and skins for covering, and a large stock of horses, some of which are very good..."[15]

The Oot-la-shoots were a friendly and amenable people. They had not been stingy or inhospitable to the Expedition. They "exchanged" worn out horses for heathy ones and sold others for not much, Capt. Clark said, *"for a few articles of merchendize."* The easy barter was pivotal for the Expedition. How could they have met the Bitterroot Mountains with worn-out horses? Could the men possibly have packed any more items over the mountains than they did? Without extra horses from the Salish, and in the steep coldness, it is doubtful. The additional colts provided emergency food when they were high and deep in the mountains and all else failed. The friendly Salish helpfulness tipped the balance for the Expedition.

They were described as *"friendly and likelyest"* in the Expedition's journals. Later in time, the Indian Agent Peter Ronan, said of them, "They were honest in dealings, quiet and amenable to their chief, brave in the field, fond of cleanliness, enemies of falsehood, and the women were known for their fidelity."[16]

The Salish were helpful to the Lewis and Clark Expedition. They provided horses for the Expedition, shared their meager food, and gave willing friendship. They told the explorers about other bands living on the Columbia, providing them with tribal intelligence and geographic information. Capt. Lewis had received from those Salish people *"such aid as they had in their power to give to assist the voyage,"*[17] as he had wished, and in the process they helped make the difference between failure or success in crossing the *"most terrible"* mountains.

Editor's Note

Early in our process of pulling together this detailed look at the portion of the Lewis and Clark Expedition's journey that involved the time it spent in the Bitterroot — and in particular wanting to focus on the historical event of their meeting with the Indians at Ross' Hole, for that moment truly serves as a symbolic turning point in our nation's western history — we realized that none of the previous published material had provided direct opportunity to the native people the Corps met in the Bitterroot, the Salish, to present their view of the encounter.

We believe that perspective, which undoubtedly would have to come out of the Salish people's rich oral history tradition given the generations that have passed since the encounter, is as vital and profound to the story of Lewis and Clark in the Bitterroot as the perspectives and insights we gain of that grand event from the journals of members of the Corps of Discovery.

Secondly, we believe that perspective, the Salish viewpoint if you will, has historical significance and cultural justification of its own. That it represents a long over-looked, even neglected dimension of complete and truthful historical perspective. Most, if not all, presentations of that encounter have come out of the white man's historical traditions, not that of the native people, the Indians Lewis and Clark met at the "Good Big Grassland," or Ross' Hole in the upper East Fork of the Bitterroot River as we call that place now.

Lastly, we also thought that the Salish perspective should be presented cleanly and directly and unfiltered. It should truly be their story, the Salish viewpoint of that historic turning point in their, and our, history. Thus, we met with representatives of the Salish Cultural Committee and invited the Salish to provide us a chapter for this book that presented their viewpoint of the encounter. In turn, we offered to present that viewpoint unedited and without comment, save two points: one, that we believe their perspective should always have been part of the written record of this story, and two, that we are grateful to them — and to Tony Incashola and Thompson R. Smith in particular — that they, too, thought it important to make the Salish viewpoint part of the written record of Lewis and Clark in the Bitterroot. Thus, we suggest you peruse the next chapter carefully. It is the Salish viewpoint of the encounter, and while all of us nowadays walk in the shadow of the Lewis and Clark Expedition, it is truly more so for the Salish and other Native Americans than most of us...

The Salish People
and the Lewis and Clark Expedition
by the Salish Culture Committee

Łu t sq̓sí....nełi ts milk̓ʷ ye stúlixʷ u es tuk̓ʷ łu malyem łu x̌ʷl sqélixʷ....x̌est es ayewti, x̌est es poxtiłši łu sxʷsixʷlts łu t sq̓si sqélixʷ. I xuk̓ʷ y e stúlixʷ, i xuk̓ʷ y e nwist, es yaʔ u x̌e. Ču łu ncaaltin.	In the old days...everywhere on this earth was the medicine of the people...They were living a good life, and their children long ago were growing up in a good way. The earth was clean, the air was clean, everything was good. There were no illnesses.

Mitch Smallsalmon (1900-1982), Pend d'Oreille elder
Salish Culture Committee Oral History Collections. Recorded April 1978.

On September 4th, 1805, a large band of the Salish people was encamped at one of the traditional places in the upper Bitterroot Valley – a place called *K̓ʷtił X̌súlexʷ*, meaning Great Clearing. Non-Indians know this place as Ross' Hole, the large upland prairie on the East Fork of the Bitterroot River. On that day nearly two hundred years ago, the people were utilizing this traditional place as countless generations of ancestors had before them – to gather chokecherries, and to pasture their fine horses on the abundant grass, before moving on toward the plains for the fall buffalo hunt. Over 30 lodges, some 400 people, and more than that number of horses, were enjoying the warm, sunny days and cold nights in this high open valley at the western base of the Pintlar Range.

While the Salish were camped at *K̓ʷtił X̌súlexʷ*, their scouts spotted a group of strange men approaching. This was the Lewis and Clark expedition.

In most non-Indian accounts, the arrival of the Lewis and Clark expedition marks the beginning of the history of Montana. But as is reflected in the Salish placenames, Lewis and Clark were in fact entering a tribal world that was older than they could have possibly imagined. For the Salish and Pend d'Oreille people, the

Photo: Salish winter camp in Bitterroot Valley, c. 1885.

The Salish People and the Lewis & Clark Expedition

encounter with the Lewis and Clark expedition, and the whole subsequent history of relations with non-Indians and the U.S. government, occupy only a small part of the most recent period of tribal history. The tribal perspective on this encounter cannot be understood without first considering the length of that history, and the depth of the tribal relationship with this place.

Tribal elders tell us that the Salish and Pend d'Oreille relationship with the land – and with the Bitterroot Valley in particular – reaches back to the earliest beginnings of human history. Linguists say that many of the names given to places in the Bitterroot, and other areas throughout the vast aboriginal territory, are among the oldest words in the Salish langauge. In fact, while some placenames, like $K^w t i\ell$ $\chi s\acute{u}lex^w$, simply describe a place, or the foods or other materials that could be found there, many other placenames come from the Coyote stories – the traditional stories of the creation of the world as we know it. From *Tmsmti* ("No Salmon," now called Lolo) to *Snetetše* ("Place of the Sleeping Baby," now called Sleeping Child Hot Springs), these are placenames rooted in the stories of how Coyote prepared the world for the human beings who were yet to come, and left the signs of his deeds upon the land. The age of those traditional stories may be reflected in their uncanny descriptions of the geologic events of the last ice age: the transformation of certain landforms, the inundation of the area beneath a great lake, the final establishment of the seasonal regime of warm and cold weather, the emergence of the animals we know today. All these events, , which geologists have dated to over 12,000 years ago, are part of the Coyote stories. Recent archaeological findings have also been dated to that distant period, including projectile points and tools in the South Fork of the Flathead River, near the center of Salish and Pend d'Oreille territory. So in part, the placenames that come from the creation stories are a linguistic record of how long the Salish have been here and a reflection of the way

of life that has sustained the people for millenia.

So when Lewis and Clark stumbled into $K^w t i\ell$ $\chi s\acute{u}lex^w$, they were much less discoverers than visitors, venturing into a very old cultural landscape. The brief period since 1800 comprises little more than one percent of the history of the Salish people

Elder John Peter Paul at $K^w t i\ell$ $\chi s\acute{u}lex^w$, September 1998.

The Salish People and the Lewis & Clark Expedition

since the ice age. Below, we have drawn a rough timeline of Salish history over that period. The arrival of Lewis and Clark is marked near the far right-hand edge.

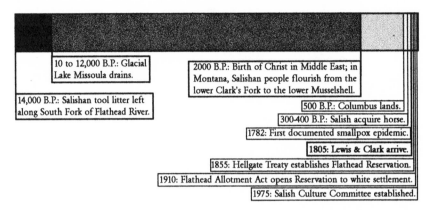

10 to 12,000 B.P.: Glacial Lake Missoula drains.	2000 B.P.: Birth of Christ in Middle East; in Montana, Salishan people flourish from the lower Clark's Fork to the lower Musselshell.
14,000 B.P.: Salishan tool litter left along South Fork of Flathead River.	

500 B.P.: Columbus lands.

300-400 B.P.: Salish acquire horse.

1782: First documented smallpox epidemic.

1805: Lewis & Clark arrive.

1855: Hellgate Treaty establishes Flathead Reservation.

1910: Flathead Allotment Act opens Reservation to white settlement.

1975: Salish Culture Committee established.

If we were to represent this timeline as a single 24-hour day, Lewis and Clark would arrive around 11:40 p.m.

We emphasize this point because it still seems that many non-Indians do not seem to believe that there were people here before the arrival of the "Corps of Discovery." The use of the word "discovery" still pervades books and films about the expedition. We can only restate what the elders have told us countless times: the Salish and Pend d'Oreille were here, a sovereign nation, a fully and richly developed culture, a people who lived by a good way of life that efficiently met their needs while taking care of, and respecting, the land they lived on.

The abundant and pristine environment the expedition encountered was not just the accidental result of a people technologically incapable of destroying it. The Salish culture in its totality, including its technology, was centered on a relationship of respect with all creatures. One of the core values that has always been taught by the elders to the younger generations is to never waste anything, to never take more than is needed; and so the people were never interested in developing the capacity to do so. The paradise that Lewis and Clark encountered was not that of an unpopulated "wilderness," but in many ways the *result* of the tribal way of life - - the product not of human absence, but of human presence. It was a way of living that nurtured, rather than depleted, the land and waters, the plants and animals, upon which we all depend for our survival on this earth.

The elders tell of how at the beginning there was a single Salish nation, which long ago had dispersed into numerous smaller groups, eventually forming the tribes we know today – Salish, Pend d'Oreille, Spokane, Colville, Couer d'Alene,

The Salish People and the Lewis & Clark Expedition

Okanagan, and others, each with its own dialect, its own specific culture, and its own territory. The lands of the Salish and Pend d'Oreille covered all of western Montana and considerable ground east of the mountains; the five or six main bands of the Salish were based at winter camps spread between the Bitterroot Valley and Three Forks. For millenia, Salish speaking peoples traveled this immense region by foot and canoe, visiting and trading with each other, following a seasonal cycle of life and expertly gathering what they needed of the earth's bounty: bitterroots, camas, buffalo, elk, deer, a wide range of fish, a plentiful array of berries, and hundreds of other foods and medicines.

In the period immediately preceding the arrival of the expedition, the Salish and Pend d'Oreille were deeply affected by a number of great changes. Between 1600 and 1700, they acquired the horse, which gave them much greater mobility, and easier access to buffalo and other foods and materials. However, the horse also increased conflict and warfare between tribes. Shortly after the establishment of the horse within the tribal cultures, epidemics of European diseases, particularly smallpox, swept through the region, having been introduced by non-Indians and then spread through inter-tribal contact. Demographers estimate that from one-third to two-thirds of the total population was eliminated in these early epidemics, and there may have been more than one; our research suggests that a one-time Salish and Pend d'Oreille population of perhaps 40,000 had been reduced to between 5,000 and 15,000 by 1800. Finally, the Blackfeet, the principal tribal adversaries of the Salish and Pend d'Oreille, acquired firearms through the Hudson's Bay Company 20 to 30 years before the Salish, whose warriors suffered heavy casualties during that period. Because of all these changes, the tribes were in a state of considerable upheaval by 1805.

Little did the Salish realize that Lewis and Clark were being sent to initiate an even more traumatic and devastating cycle of change among the people. In his instructions to Meriwether Lewis, President Thomas Jefferson stated that "The object of your mission is to explore the Missouri river," and to find the best water route to the Pacific ocean, "for the purposes of commerce." In his message to Congress seeking funding for the expedition, Jefferson presented scientific inquiry as merely "incidental" and "an additional gratification." The law subsequently passed by Congress was entitled "An Act making an appropriation for extending the external commerce of the United States." Lewis and Clark, in short, were primarily sent west to lay the groundwork for the establishment of an American claim to the emerging fur trade in the West. For native people, this meant the claiming of Indian land, the cataloguing of Indian resources, and finally the imposition of a fundamentallly

The Salish People and the Lewis & Clark Expedition

different way of life.

The Salish were unaware of Lewis and Clark's full objectives, and so gave them a great deal of help during their brief encounter. The expedition's stock was exhausted, and the people gifted them with a dozen of their "ellegant horses," as Clark described them. In return, the Salish accepted seven lame animals and a few small gifts. The tribe also gave the strangers food from their dried stores, robes, and a dozen pack saddles – altogether, goods representing a very great amount of labor, work that had been carried out by Salish women over countless days and months in the previous year.

The Salish horses may well have saved the lives of at least some members of the expedition. From *Kʷtił X̱súlexʷ*, the party proceeded north through the Bitterroot Valley until they reached Lolo Creek, where they moved on toward Idaho over the Bitterroot Mountains. They didn't know the trail and moved slowly through deep snows and bitter cold. For over a week they were forced to subsist on the meat of the Salish horses. As Lewis wrote after his return,

"....most fortunately on our way within the Mountains we met with a travelling Band of the Tushopahs going to the Plains of the Missesourii in quest of Buffaloe & obtained from them an accession of 7 Horses to our former Stock exchanging at the same time 10 or 12 to great advantage; this ultimately proved of infinite Service to us as we were compelled to subsist on Horse Beef & Dogs previous to our arrival in the navigable [part?] of the Kooskooskee. I have not the leisure at this moment to state all those difficulties which we encountered in our Passage over these Mountains – suffice it to say we suffered everything Cold, Hunger, & Fatigue could impart, or the Keenest Anxiety excited for the fate of Expedition in which our whole Souls were embarked."

The Salish People and the Lewis & Clark Expedition

Salish Oral Traditions
Relating to the Encounter with Lewis and Clark

Pete Beaverhead (1899-1975), one of the great Pend d'Oreille oral historians of his generation, told the following account a few months before his death in 1975. Mr. Beaverhead's narrative is probably less precise than some others in its historical detail; he blurs the encounter with Lewis and Clark with the much earlier native encounters with Columbus, and the much later implementation of the allotment act on the Flathead Reservation. But this is an instructive blurring. Mr. Beaverhead is telling us that these are all chapters of the same story; all are examples of the gradual process of non-Indian invasion of Indian lands and of the arrogance of non-Indian explorers.

The second passage, told in 1977 by Mitch Smallsalmon (1900-1982), also a Pend d'Oreille elder who possessed great knowledge of the tribe's history and culture, echoes Mr. Beaverhead in its commentary on the act of planting a flag and laying claim to native land.

🐃 🐃 🐃 🐃

"They hadn't seen our land yet, and they had already sold it."
Pete Beaverhead

Kʷem̓t łihé yeʔs meyy̓em̓. Kʷem̓t łu kʼłpáʔx̣nten, čnńté tł čełlnq̓ʷoq̓í sm̓x̣ʷop u č m̓słnq̓ʷoq̓í či č či. U n̓pʌmú ec̓x̣ey̓ łu i t mi. Łu iqs c meyy̓é łu in qnqené, i sł̓síle, i sx̣px̣epiyé, in ilaw̓iyes, t̓pt̓úpiyes. Łu es nmícinm̓s.... Kʷem̓t tl še cx̣uy, yecčč̓ʔé, u wičis łu suyapi. Nq̓ʷon̓mis łu suyapi, i pqpiq,

This is what I am telling. Then when I thought about it, I think it is about three hundred or four hundred snows ago, and even beyond that time, is what I am telling you about. They are true stories.

These stories were interpreted to my paternal grandmothers, my maternal grandfathers, and my paternal grandfathers by their great-great-grandparents, their great-grandparents a long time ago. These are true stories.... Then, as time went by, the Indians seen the whiteman and felt pity for them, because their faces were pale, white-

The Salish People and the Lewis & Clark Expedition

u es upupus.
Ec̣x̣lús tes č łix̌ʷmú
x̌ʷoł is piq i kʷils.
Kʷemt łu čicntm łu t suyapi
kʷ ƛe cnteʔšlš łu suyapi, kʷemt
x̌ʷpx̌ʷépis łu ep
spum łu sicm, še kʷłsx̌ʷmeys i
šeỷ u qs łaqqi.
Cuti łu ilimix̌ʷm, "N̓em
x̌ʷpx̌ʷépntp ci sicm,
ci ep spum m i šeỷ
m łaqq. X̌ʷa es siyuỷti,
es nte es siyuỷti,
u i pqpiqs."
Tl še es ctax̌ʷlú cx̌ʷuy
u miip epł
nččx̌ʷcox̌ʷepletn łu
suyapi. Kʷ łu qs
cniʔekʷ
i es š̓it
qs cniʔekʷmi łu
suyapi u ƛe qe
tumistmłt łu qe
s̓tulix̌ʷ łu i
amotqn, "Cuỷs kʷ aqs
x̌ʷučstm t ƛiyéʔ čiqs
ƛemi t s̓tulix̌ʷ.
Ep s̓tulix̌ʷ. Łu n̓e čin wičm t
s̓tulix̌ʷ," kʷemt cuỷs łu amotqis,
łu *king*, "n̓em aqł s̓tulix̌ʷ."
Kʷemt łi i, i cỷú qe es wičłt
łu qe s̓tulix̌ʷ u ƛe qe tumistmłt.
Kʷemt cntešlš u
nṣ̓tulex̌ʷm
t sccacé.
U kʷemt x̌ʷa ecx̣ey qe
kʷłx̌ʷuupmis.

looking, and they had beards. The white men looked as if they were cold because their faces were pale and red. Then, when the Indians met the whiteman (because they had already landed), then the Indians spread out their fur blankets and motioned to the white men to sit on the blankets. Their chief told them to spread out the fur blankets so that the white men can sit on them, because maybe they are cold. The Indians thought the white men were cold because they were white-faced.

From that time on, it became known that the whites had laws. Right then, when the white men were to come across the ocean for the first time, our land had already been sold by them to the Government. The whiteman told the Government people, "You give me a ship to go across to look for some land. There is land over there. If we find some land," they told the Government, their king, "it will be your land."

They hadn't seen our land yet, and they had already sold it.

The whiteman crossed and landed. They stuck pole &flag in the ground, claiming the land.

We lost our land, they beat us out of it.

Pete Beaverhead, age 9

The Salish People and the Lewis & Clark Expedition

Łu es šʔi sqelixʷ wičis, k̓ʷemt
k̓ʷnk̓ʷenštm t sq̓lq̓alé,
t sctk̓ʷłik̓ʷ.
šey̓ łu nx̣eselsmis, lemtmis,
łu t sqelixʷ.
K̓ʷemt č šey̓ u qe nunx̣ʷené.
K̓ʷemt es miiiilk̓ʷ yetłx̣ʷa ye
s̓tulixʷ, qe s̓tulixʷ ye es čsunk̓ʷ,
u c̓x̣ey̓ t lčntes x̣ʷoi̓ qe nplé.
Qe k̓ʷix̣qeyx̣ʷłit łu pn tl qe
snici̓cítn u qe cułt. Łu t
suyapi, "Ihé łu aqs sqalixʷulexʷ,
aqł nlcitn."
U qe eł łsxʷsux̣ʷmešlš tes
heʔheʔnmłʔú acre, t qeq̓ s̓tulixʷ,
t qeq̓ł čmšté. "Qe c̓ułs ihé łu
aqł čmšté, aqł s̓tulixʷ." K̓ʷemt
n̓x̣ʷʔit, če k̓ʷtnúlexʷ łu
sm̓ʔawúlexʷ u eł k̓ʷulis łu t
suyapi u qe tumistmłls,
x̣ʷicšmis, nʔaysis łu t suyapi. U
c̓npilš u qe p̓inmłt.
K̓ʷ unexʷ č qeq̓s šimi
či eighty acres, qeq̓s
nlcitn. Hoy čtaxʷlé
n̓ʔaysis łu t suyapi, łu
s̓tlt̓ulixʷ, qe tuumistmntm u
p̓ut̓ u qes....

The first Indians they saw, the whites showed the Indians necklaces, string, or something; the Indians liked them. They enjoyed the jewelry.

We believed their words.

This land all over, this island – today, the whiteman has tied it up for us. They chased us away from our own land, our homes. The whiteman told us, "This is to be your Indian land, your Reservation. It is where you will live."

Then they set it up, surveyed it, in 80 acres, to be our land, to be our homestead. "This is here is your homestead, your land." There were many acres left over, and they found a way so that we sold the land, so that it was given, it was bought by the whiteman. And they came in and crowded us out.

It is the truth, our land was made into eighty acres, for our place to live. Now today it has been bought by the whiteman, all our land, we sold it, and it is almost all gone...

The Salish People and the Lewis & Clark Expedition

🐃 🐃 🐃 🐃

"When he got off his ship he put his flag in the ground....just like he put a brand on this land."
Mitch Smallsalmon

Kʷemt i šeẏ u es čšín, u łu x̣ʷa i čen u ax̣eẏ u, łu es š̓ʔí suyá čxʷuy, łu es čustm̓ *Columbus*. Kʷemt łu cntešlš, u wičis ye s̓tulixʷ, t̓ipncú łu ti ƛiyés u n̓š̓tulexʷis łu sččacé. Čx̣ey es lem̓ti, es lem̓ti tixʷ s̓tulixʷ. U wičis, we wičis ye sqelixʷ, tutupiyewt, es t̓ʔaccx̣. Kʷemt ta es misten̓, ta čiqs ču łu, łu i šeẏ u ečx̣eẏ łu sck̓ʷípaxs łu suyá. Kʷemt čk̓ʷ̓iči u ƛe, ƛe píx̣is ye s̓tulixʷ. ƛe wičm̓ t qs s̓tulixʷs, u ta x̣ʷa es k̓ʷestc či, cniłč snččxʷepls, łu čx̣ey qs n̓čmełxʷ ye t qe sqelixʷ, kʷ łu t s̓tulixʷ, čx̣eẏ ta es čsewplís čmi nełi. Kʷemt č snččxʷepletis u t̓k̓ʷuntes.

Mitch Smallsalmon, c. 1980

Then that's when people said the first whiteman here came from what you call Columbus. When he came across to see this land, when he got off his ship, he put his flag in the ground. I guess same as saying he was glad to have and own some land.

He did see the Indians standing in groups all staring at him, but I'm not going to say what was on their minds – I mean, about the white people.

Then, just as soon as he was on the ground, just like he put a brand on this land. He found the land, but I don't think he carried any kind of important papers about laws. And to come here and take away and claim our Indian land – he didn't even have permission from anyone to take our land. But I guess they thought they'd just go ahead and use their own laws.

🐃 🐃 🐃 🐃

The Salish People and the Lewis & Clark Expedition

Other Salish Accounts of Lewis and Clark:
Misunderstanding and Miscommunication

Many non-Indian historians and filmmakers have depicted the encounter between Indian people and the Lewis and Clark expedition as a story of respectful cultural exchange and mutual understanding.

In fact, when we listen to the elders' stories, or even when we carefully read some of the expedition journals, the encounters between Lewis and Clark and the native people seem marked primarily by misunderstanding and miscommunicaiton. Private Joseph Whitehouse noted, in regard to the expedition's interaction with the Salish, that "we could not talk with them as much as we wish, for all that we Say has to go through 6 languages before it gits to them and it is hard to make them understand all what we Say." Whitehouse said the expedition members found the Salish language very difficult, so they figured the Salish must be the "Welsh Indians," drawing on an old myth about a group of Welsh people who had sailed to North America and settled on the upper Missouri river.

Clearly, there was misunderstanding on both sides. As the elders have told us, the Salish thought the expedition members must have been in mourning, since their hair was cut short. They thought their pale pink skin was due to being cold. They thought the African-American member of the expedition, York, was a warrior who had painted himself black in preparation for war.

Yet there is also a crucial difference here. The Salish accounts focus on the misunderstanding. They make a point of how they misinterpreted what they saw. The non-Indian accounts, and especially the later histories of the expedition, downplay that misunderstanding or even deny it. It is important for us to think about why this is so. The romantic glow of Lewis and Clark rests in part on the myth that Indian people welcomed the expedition in the full knowledge of their intentions.

In fact, we might wonder whether the very survival of the expedition was the product of Salish misunderstanding. As most of the elders' accounts make clear, the first decision of the chief, *Četl Sqey̓mi*, (Three Eagles), was whether the strange party constituted a threat to the people's well-being. He decided they were not. Although they seemed to be a war party, they seemed pitiful and perhaps in mourning. As Pete Beaverhead said, the Salish "believed their words" of friendship. *Četl Sqey̓mi* decided they should take the strangers in and feed them, rather than wipe them out. By Lewis' reckoning, the Salish had a force of about 80 warriors at *Kʷtił X̌súlexʷ*.

The Salish People and the Lewis & Clark Expedition

Pierre Pichette (1877-1955), a reknowned tribal oral historian, related the following story in 1953 to Ella Clark, a non-Indian researcher. Clark apparently did not record the interview, so we rely on her recounting of it. She mentions no interpreter; it is possible that Pichette spoke in English. The story was published in Clark's *Indian Legends from the Northern Rockies* (Norman: Oklahoma University Press, 1966).

"The chief immediately sent his warriors to meet the strange men and to bring them to camp safely."
Pierre Pichette *via* Ella Clark

Our people were camped in a kind of prairie along the Bitterroot River, a few miles upstream from the Medicine Tree. The place is called Ross's Hole now; the Indians then called it *Cutl-kkh-pooh.*[1] They kept close watch over their camps in those days and always had scouts out because they feared an attack by an enemy tribe. One day two scouts came back to report that they had seen some human beings who were very different from any they had known. Most of the strangers had pale skins, and their clothing was altogether different from anything the Indians wore.

"There were seven of them," the scouts told Chief Three Eagles (Tchliska-e-mee). "They have little packs on their backs, maybe provisions or clothing."

The chief immediately sent his warriors to meet the strange men and to bring them to camp safely.

"Do no harm to them," he warned his men. "Do no harm to them at all. Bring them to me safely."

So the strangers were brought into the camp. All the tipis were arranged in a circle in our camps, with an open space in the center. The people gathered there in the middle of the camping place, and so, when the warriors brought the strange men in, they were seen by the whole tribe. The Indians could not understand who the seven men were, but they knew they were human beings.

Chief Three Eagles ordered buffalo robes to be brought and to be spread in the gathering place. By signs, he told the strangers to sit on the robes. The men were a puzzling sight to all the Indians surrounding them.

After the white men had sat down, they took their little packs off their backs. The chief looked through their packs and then began to explain to the people.

---

1. Linguistic & ethnogeographic research with tribal elders suggests Clark was apparently trying to spell Kʷtit Xsúlexʷ, meaning Great Clearing, as spelled in the modern International Phonetic Alphabet.

The Salish People and the Lewis & Clark Expedition

Pierre Pichette

"I think they have had a narrow escape from their enemies. All their belongings were taken away by the enemy. That's why there is so little in their packs. Maybe the rest of the tribe were killed. Maybe that is why there are only seven of them. These men must be very hungry, perhaps starving. And see how poor and torn their clothes are." The chief ordered food to be brought to them□ dried buffalo meat and dried roots. He ordered clothing also to be brought to them – buckskins and light buffalo robes that were used for clothing.

One of the strange men was black. He had painted himself in charcoal, my people thought. In those days it was the custom for warriors, when returning home from battle, to prepare themselves before reaching camp. Those who had been brave and fearless, the victorious ones in battle, painted themselves in charcoal. When the warriors returned to their camp, people knew at once which ones had been brave on the warpath. So the black man, they thought, had been the bravest of this party.

All the men had short hair. So our people thought that the seven were in mourning for the rest of the party who had been slaughtered. It was the custom for mourners to cut their hair.

By signs, Chief Three Eagles and his counselors came to a little understanding with the white men. Then the chief said to his people, "This party is the first of this kind of people we have ever seen. They have been brought in safely. I want them taken out safely. I want you warriors to go with them part of the way to make sure that they leave our country without harm."

So by the chief's orders, a group of young warriors accompanied the white men to the edge of the Salish country. They went with the strangers down the river from Ross's Hole and up to Lolo Pass. The white men went on from there.

They did not take with them the robes and clothing Chief Three Eagles had given them. Perhaps the white men did not understand that they were gifts.

In 1953, Ella Clark also interviewed Sophie Moiese (1866-1960), one of the most culturally knowledgeable elders of the Bitterroot Salish. As with the interview with Pierre Pichette, Clark apparently did not record the story, so we do not have the original words spoken by Moiese. Moiese spoke in Salish, and Clark relied on Louie Pierre for translation and interpretation. This story was also published in *Indian Legends from the Northern Rockies*.

- 12 -

The Salish People and the Lewis & Clark Expedition

About 1908 or 1909, the photographer Edward S. Curtis interviewed Salish people about Lewis and Clark while gathering material for his multi-volume work, *The North American Indian* (Cambridge, Mass., 1907-1930; Johnson Reprint Corporation, New York, 1976). (Vol. VII (1911), p. 44).

"The chief said: "They do not have robes to sit on....Bring them some robes."
Tribal account recorded by Edward S. Curtis

The two captains advanced and shook hands with the chief, who commanded his people to refrain from any evil-doing toward them. The white men removed their pack-saddles from their horses and sat down on the ground. The chief said: "They do not have robes to sit on. Some Indians have stolen them. Bring them some robes." Buffalo-skins were brought, but instead of sitting on them, the white men threw them about their shoulders. One of them had a black face, and the Indians said among themselves, "See, his face is painted black! They are going to have a scalp-dance!"

The accounts of Pierre Pichette, Sophie Moiese, and the unnamed storyteller recorded by Edward Curtis provide vivid examples of the confusion -- and sometimes conflict -- that often arose around the exchange of goods. Mr. Pichette reports that the expedition members did not take the robes that had been given them. Mrs. Moiese notes that they didn't eat the dried meat and baked camas that was set before them. It is a reflection of the generosity of spirit of both Pichette and Moiese that they offer charitable explanations for actions that are usually considered highly offensive in tribal culture. Pichette speculates that "perhaps the white men did not understand that they were gifts." Moiese offers that they thought the meat "was

The Salish People and the Lewis & Clark Expedition

About 1908 or 1909, the photographer Edward S. Curtis interviewed Salish people about Lewis and Clark while gathering matierial for his mutli-volume work, *The North American Indian* (Cambridge, Mass., 1907-1930; Johnson Reprint Corporation, New York, 1976). (Vol. VII (1911), p. 44).

"The chief said: "They do not have robes to sit on....Bring them some robes."
Tribal account recorded by Edward S. Curtis

The two captains advanced and shook hands with the chief, who commanded his people to refrain from any evil-doing toward them. The white men removed their pack-saddles from their horses and sat down on the ground. The chief said: "They do not have robes to sit on. Some Indians have stolen them. Bring them some robes." Buffalo-skins were brought, but instead of sitting on them, the white men threw them about their shoulders. One of them had a black face, and the Indians said among themselves, "See, his face is painted black! They are going to have a scalp-dance!"

While the following account is one of the oldest we have, it comes to us third or fourth-hand. It was written down by Jerome D'Aste, a Jesuit priest at the St. Ignatius Mission, and subsequently published by O.D. Wheeler in *The Trail of Lewis and Clark, 1804-1904*, Vol. II (1904: New York and London: G.P. Putnam's Sons, the Knickerbocker Press; repr. AMS Press, Inc., New York, 1976, pp. 65-68.) While compiling his book on Lewis and Clark, Wheeler asked his "friend Father D'Aste" if he could obtain the story of the Salish encounter of the expedition from an elder he'd heard about – "an old and reliable Indian, Francois."

D'Aste wrote back to Wheeler on September 5, 1899. He had been told the story three days earlier by Francois Saxa, whom D'Aste described as having "the enviable reputation among the settler of being a truthful man, on whose words they could depend." According to D'Aste, Saxa said he had been told about the Salish encounter with the Lewis and Clark expedition by "old Agnes, the wife of Chief Victor and stepmother of Charlot.... He said he remembered very well what the old Agnes related to the Indians about that

The Salish People and the Lewis & Clark Expedition

historical meeting."

It is the last stage of the story's transmission that raises the most questions, for while tribal oral traditions often maintained high standards of fidelity in their retelling across generations, its passage to D'Aste required a process of translation both of language and of culture. Nevertheless, with a grain of salt, we print the account – the story of Victor's widow, as told to Francois Saxa, filtered through Jerome D'Aste, S.J., and finally printed by O.D. Wheeler, who said he himself made "a change here and there."

"At a distance he saw a party of about twenty men traveling toward his camp."

Francois Saxa's account of the story told by Agnes, Chief Victor's widow, *via* Jerome D'Aste, S.J., and O.D. Wheeler

The Flathead Indians were camping at Ross's Hole, or Ross's fork, at the head of the Bitterroot valley, when one day the old chief, Three Eagles, the father of Chief Victor and grandfather of Charlot, left the camp to go scouting the country, fearing there might be some Indian enemies around with the intent to steal horses, as it was done then very frequently. He saw at a distance Lewis and Clark's party, about twenty men, each man leading two pack horses, except two, who were riding ahead, who were Lewis and Clark. The old chief, seeing that these men wore no blankets, did not know what to think of them. It was the first time he had met men without blankets. What kind of beings could they be? The first thought was that they were a party of men who, traveling, had been robbed by some Indians of their blankets. He went back to his people and, reporting to them what he had seen, he gave orders that all the horses should be driven in and watched, for fear the party he had seen might be on a stealing expedition. He then went back toward the party of strange beings, and, hiding himself in the timber, watched them.

When they came to the open prairie he noticed that they traveled slowly and unconcerned, all together, the two leaders going ahead of the party and looking around, as if surveying the country and consulting with their men. He thought within himself. These must be two chiefs; but what can they be after? To make things more complicated for the old chief, there was a colored man in the party. What can this man be? When the Indians were going to the buffalo hunt they had

The Salish People and the Lewis & Clark Expedition

a custom, if any sign would appear of their enemies hiding around, to have a *war dance* to encourage one another to fight and be brave. For this dance, the Indian warriors would paint themselves, some in red, some in yellow, some in black, etc, and from the color each had chosen to paint himself his name was called. The black face, thought the old chief, must surely be a man who painted his face black in sign of war. The party must have had a fight with some hostile Indians and escaped from their enemies, losing only their blankets.

Seeing that the strangers were traveling in the direction of his camp, the old chief went back to his people and told them to keep quiet and wait for the party to come near. From the easy and unconcerned way the strange beings were traveling, the Indians inferred they had no intention to fight or to injure them. Hence, when they saw the strangers advancing, in the same manner, toward them, and were already near their camp, the Indians did not move, but kept watching. When the two leaders of the party, coming to the Indian camp, showed friendship to the Indians, there was a universal shaking of hands. The chief then gave orders to the Indians to bring in the best buffalo hides, one for each man to sit on, and the best buffalo robes also, one for each man to use as a blanket. Then the two leaders, observing that the Indians were using, for smoking, the leaves of some plant, a plant very much alike to our tobacco plant, asked for some and filled their pipes; but as soon as they tried to smoke, they pronounced the *Indian tobacco* no good. Cutting some of their own tobacco they gave it to the Indians, telling them to fill their pipes with it. But it was too much for them, who had never tried the American weed, and all began to cough, with great delight to the party. Then the two leaders asked the Indians for some Kinnickinnick, mixed it with the tobacco, and gave again to the Indians the prepared weed to smoke. This time the Indians found it excellent, and in their way thanked the men whom they now believed a friendly party. On their side the whites, seeing the friendly dispositions of the Indians, decided to camp right there, and they began to unpack their horses, giving the Indians to understand that they also had blankets in their packs, but that they used them only to sleep in, and gave them back the robes. The Indians were soon out of their wits when they saw some of the men packing on their shoulders pretty good sized logs for their camp fires, and conceived a great idea of the power of the white man. All went on friendly, and after three days they started off, directed to Lolo fork's trail by the Indians, as the best way to go to the Nez Percés' country.

I am yours respectfully, J. D'Aste, S.J.

The Salish People and the Lewis & Clark Expedition

Jerome D'Aste was not the only missionary who relayed some version of the tribal stories of Lewis and Clark. In 1923, Mother Angela Lincoln published *Life of the Rev. Mother Amadeus of the Heart of Jesus: Foundress of the Ursuline Missions of Montana and Alaska*, a heroizing account of Amadeus's work. Following is Lincoln's retelling of Mother Amadeus' retelling of what was told to her by an elder Salish woman known to the church as "Old Eugenie."

"....they wondered at the unseemly trousers, and pityingly gave them blankets to cover their legs...."
Old Eugenie *via* Mother Amadeus & Mother Angela Lincoln

Captain Lewis and Captain Clark were....the first white men to enter the present limits of the State of Montana. Old Eugenie, who was still living in 1890, when Mother Amadeus opened the Mission at St. Ignatius, remembered the reverence with which the Indians carried about the first white men they had ever seen, how they wondered at the unseemly trousers, and pityingly gave them blankets to cover their legs before they suffered them to treat with Indian dignitaries....

....Old Eugenie, who lived to be one hundred years old....told that when Lewis and Clark came, they gave the Flatheads a present of a bell and a looking glass. This latter the chief poetically mistook to be the soul. He stored his treasure jealously away in his own "tepee," and when the young girls of the tribe gathered about him on Saturday nights, as they regularly did, being summoned by the bell to keep the weekly vigil and to watch for the rising of the sun on the seventh morning, they were admitted, one by one, to look each at her own soul – *i.e.,* her face in the glass, and when thus purified, by prayer and self-contemplation, they beheld the first streaks of dawn athwart proud McDonald, they rose, joined their hands above their heads, and then prostrated on the ground face downward, and prayed aloud, each one cryinig out the needs of her soul.

There is something noble in our Indians, even in their poor benighted paganism.

The Salish People and the Lewis & Clark Expedition

Our next account was told by a Salish woman named Ochanee to Peter Ronan, U.S. Indian Agent on the Flathead Reservation from 1877 until his death in 1893. Ochanee's account appeared in Ronan's *History of the Flathead Indians* (Minneapolis: Ross & Haines, 1890), a mix of useful fact and apparent efforts by Ronan to secure a positive image for himself in the history books.

"Captain Clarke took unto himself a Flathead woman.
One son was the result of this union...."
Ochanee, via Peter Ronan, 1890

At the date of this writing, May 1890, there still lives at St. Ignatius mission, on the Flathead reservation, an old Indian woman named Ochanee, who distinctly remembers, and relates in the Indian language the advent of those two great captains, with their followers, into the Flathead camp in the Bitter Root valley, and the great astonishment it created among the Indians.

The explorers crossed over the Big Hole Mountains and arrived at the Flathead camp in the Bitter Root valley in the year 1804. Ochanee claims to have been about 13 years of age at that date. She is a lively old woman, and still has all of her mental faculties, and can describe camps, scenes and events which are vividly portrayed in the published reports of Lewis and Clark descriptive of the Flathead and Nez Perce Indians, who were then hunting and camping together.

During the stay of the explorers in the Flathead camp Captain Clarke took unto himself a Flathead woman. One son was the result of this union, and he was baptised after the missionaries came to Bitter Root valley and named Peter Clarke. This halfbreed lived to a ripe age, and was well known to many of Montana's early settlers. He died about six years ago and left a son, who was christened at St. Mary's mission to the name of Zachariah, and pronounced Sacalee by the Indians. The latter has a son three years of age, whom it is claimed by the Indians, indirect descent, to be the great grandson of the renowned Captain Clarke.

The Salish People and the Lewis & Clark Expedition

Perhaps the most interesting detail in this account is Ochanee's confirmation of the impregnation of an Indian woman by William Clark. While she is here said to have been a Salish woman, the expedition journals suggest she was from the Nez Perce people. In any case, it is clear that the descendants of Clark's son lived on the Flathead Reservation. And there is further evidence of this in the historical record. Nearly ninety years after the Salish hosted the expedition at Kʷtiɫ Xsúlexʷ, the Commissioner of Indian Affairs received the mandatory monthly report from Ronan (National Archives, RG 75, BIA LR 1893-1837). The report, dated January 4th, 1893, reads in part:

Sir: At the beginning of the New Year, it is my pleasant duty to report for the month of December....

A young Indian called Sacalee Clarke, the reputed grandson of Captain Clarke, the explorer, was killed at Arlee station, on the reservation, on the night of December 27th, by attempting, it is supposed, to get off the train while in motion.....

Very respectfully,
Your obedient servant
Peter Ronan, United States Indian Agent.
* * * *

Many non-Indian historians have celebrated courage and toughness exhibited by Lewis and Clark during their two-year journey. But as Pete Beaverhead told us at the beginning of this chapter, for the Salish and Pend d'Oreille, the expedition stands as yet another example of early non-Indians laying claim to a land that was never theirs. In so doing, they prepared the way for great, unjustified injury to the native people of this area.

When Lewis returned to St. Louis in September 1806, he immediately wrote to President Jefferson. Lewis' letter carried eastward the first information from the expedition – and it focused, most of all, on the potential of the region for a booming American fur trade:

"....We view this passage across the Continent as affording immence advantages to the fur trade....The Missouri and all it's branches from the Chyenne upwards abound more in beaver and Common Otter, than any other streams on earth, particularly that portion of them lying within the Rocky Mountains....Although the Columbia dose not as much as the Missouri abound in beaver and Otter....it....would furnish a valuable fur trade....There might be collected considerable quantities of the skins of three speceis of bear affording a great variety of colours and of superior delicacy, those also of the tyger cat, several species of fox, martin and several other...."

The Salish People and the Lewis & Clark Expedition

As Jefferson had hoped, the information provided by Lewis and Clark helped ignite an explosion of American fur trade activity throughout the upper Missouri and Columbia drainages. Over the following decades, fur traders would use the expedition's published journals as guides to their systematic exploitation of the region. Although some tribes, particularly in Canada, participated intensively in trapping beaver and other animals, most Indian people in the Northwest took part in a sporadic way. For the Salish, Pend d'Oreille, and other tribes, the fur trade supplemented, rather than replaced, their traditional way of life. In fact, the journals of fur traders are riddled with instances of conflict and confrontation with tribes who opposed the looting of their resources. As the devastating ecological effects of the trade rippled across the region, and as the animals that helped sustain the people became ever scarcer, the tribes themselves became poorer and more dependent on the white man's way of life. By 1840, the height of the fur trade had passed due to the extermination of so many animals.

After 1840, and particuarly after the establishment of Montana Territory in 1864, conditions became even more difficult, in many ways, for tribal people in the region. It could be said that the expedition's goal of transcontinental commerce found its ultimate realization in 1883 with the construction of the Northern Pacific Railroad through the region, and through the Flathead Reservation itself, over the bitter objections of tribal leaders. The railroad's completion, and the simultaneous elimination of the great buffalo herds, fundamentally changed the balance of power in western Montana and marginalized the Indian way of life that had defined the region for thousands of years. And it was on this same railroad, as we have seen, that William Clark's Salish grandson, Sacalee Clark, tragically died in December 1892.

Yet there is also hope to be taken from this history. Throughout these years, the Salish, the Pend d'Oreille, and the Kootenai nations, and many non-Indians in the region, have continued to work for a different kind of relationship - - one built on honesty, consideration, and the honoring of solemn obligations. Part of that effort has involved the inquiry into our collective and mutual history for purposes not of glorification or of creating heroes, but of understanding, of the search for the truth, of looking for the origins of our present condition. Perhaps this chapter, in itself, may be seen as a promising example of this endeavor. Over the past two hundred years, this kind of cross-cultural dialogue has been far too infrequent. Now, in an increasing number of venues, tribal points of view are being heard. It is on this basis of respect that we can work together to make the history of the next two centuries more humane and more just.

CHAPTER SIX

THROUGH THE BITTERROOT VALLEY

F RIDAY, SEPTEMBER 6, 1805. Time for departure. The Indians broke camp preparing to travel east over their pass (Gibbons Pass) to the Big Hole basin where they planned to rendezvous with their allies at the Three Forks. It was time to hunt buffalo. What a spectacle! Five hundred horses, four hundred people and numerous barking dogs, all excited and anxious to start the journey to meet their friends, exchange stories, and hunt the winter's food supply. Surely at night by the campfires they would tell of the white men who came to them, and conjecture what their appearance meant.

Dr. Swanzey tells us that "as one leaves the vicinity of the campsite of September 4 and 5 and looks southward, and shortly after leaving the treeless area, Indian Trees Campground is to the right. The Indians removed the bark of Ponderosa Pine trees then scraped the cambium layer as a source of food, a practice which the Indians continued there until the early 1920's. The scars are still plainly visible. It is also where the East and West forks of Camp Creek join, and where the Corps had a sparing lunch on September 4 just before their meeting with the Flathead encampment."[1]

The Corps, too, was anxious to push on through the valley toward its goal, the trail of the Nez Perce, which they understood to be about four nights north. Time was a factor as was the season. With growing anxiety the men watched the looming Bitterroot mountains on their left. Craggy cliffs and slopes jutted skyward like the sharp pointed teeth in the jaw of an old weathered crone. Perhaps Lewis was remembering that day last August when he looked over those endless mountain ranges and realized that his dream of a short and easy portage to the Columbia basin and hence to the Pacific Ocean had disappeared like the smoke from the Indian tepees. Once more, the Corps of Discovery would have to face the mountains which seemed determined to challenge all the strength, ingenuity and determination of the members of the Expedition.

The journal keepers reported, *"a clear cold morning,"* which the men spent loading and redistributing the packs. The worn-out Shoshone horses were given lighter loads, the excess baggage was transferred to the fresh Salish horses. By mid-afternoon the travelers were again on their way. Clark reported that *"Small Creek from the North all three forks Comeing together below our Camp at which place the Mountains Close on each Side of the river, ...Crossed a Mountain and place the Indians had Encamped two days before. We Proceeded on down the River which is 30 yds wide Shallow & Stoney Crossing it Several times & Encamped in a Small bottom on the right side, rained this evening nothing to eate but berries, our flour out, and but little Corn. Struck the river Several miles down, at which point crossed a Small river from the right ..."* [2] This camp was northeast of Sula on the East Fork of the Bitterroot and is also known as Flour Camp.

The Corps now traveled up Cameron Creek, crossed over a low saddle of Sula Peak and down Spring Gulch to the East Fork of the Bitterroot River.

Dr. Swanzey asks, "Why didn't they just go down the East Fork instead of a circuitous route?" He answers, "Simple. The East Fork was impassible due to years of accumulated debris and a large rock cliff (Jim Hell Rock) impinging the channel. Why hadn't the Indians cleaned it out? Indians did not build trails; Indians did not maintain trails. There is always another way to get from here to there. How did Jim Hell Rock get its name? In 1878 a group of engineers came up the East Fork seeking to build a road to Bannack. Some Indians were camped at Rattlesnake Gulch along with an Indian trapper, Delaware Jim. When asked about the passage ahead Delaware Jim told the engineers about the big rock and "You have a hell of a time getting around it." The engineers went to see. There was a tree leaning against it. One man climbed up and painted 'Jim Hell Rock'. Eventually much blasting reduced the rock to its present size." The early settlers, circa 1872, cleaned out the debris, but it took 18 crossings to get to Ross' Hole and the road to Bannack never was built. "[3]

Joseph Whitehouse wrote, *"We had nothing to eat except a little parched corn meal, but our party are all contented.* "[4] They camped that night at Beam Flat, the first really wide spot in the valley.

Question: The men of the Corps of Discovery were hungry. These meat eaters were accustomed to nine to ten pounds of meat a day. Why were the hunters unable to bring back enough meat for the troops? There is plenty of game in the Bitterroot Mountains today, but two hundred years ago there wasn't. The deer population was low because of natural predators; the wolf, coyote, mountain lion and also the Indians. The predators were hunted down and eliminated by the settlers of the 1880's and 1900's and, in the case of the Indians, removed. Elk were practically unheard of in the lower valley until after 1900, although some did trickle across the Divide from Idaho. In 1912, three carloads of elk were shipped to the valley from Yellowstone National Park. Money was raised by a local subscription campaign. Thirty head, which were allocated to Stevensville, were turned loose on Burnt Fork. Another carload for Hamilton were relocated on Gird Creek. Willow Creek received the carload for Corvallis and Woodside.[5] Hunting of big game is now regulated and seasonal. Also, deer prefer open places to dense forests. When homeowners clear the land, they also establish deer habitat.

Saturday, September 7, 1805. Again the day was cold, cloudy dark and drizzly. The travelers proceeded down the East Fork of the Bitterroot to its junction with the West Fork and the formation of the Bitterroot River.

The Indians called the river *spe'tlemen* meaning "place of the bitterroot". The river's name in Salish became *spitlem seukm*, which means "water of the bitterroot." Lewis named the river Clark's River. Alexander Ross referred to it as Cortine's Fork of the Piegan; David Thompson called it the Southern Branch of the Flathead. Apparently the first non-Indian to call it Bitter Root was explorer Warren A. Ferris during the 1830's. Father DeSmet renamed it the St. Mary's River (along with the valley and the mountain) in 1841. In 1852 Major John Owen, founder of Fort Owen trading post, was referring to it as the Bitter Root River. In 1898 the Forest Service mapmakers gave the present one-word spelling, Bitterroot. Some

Waterways named by Lewis and Clark
Sept 4, 1805 — Sept 12, 1805
June 29, 1806 — July 5, 1806

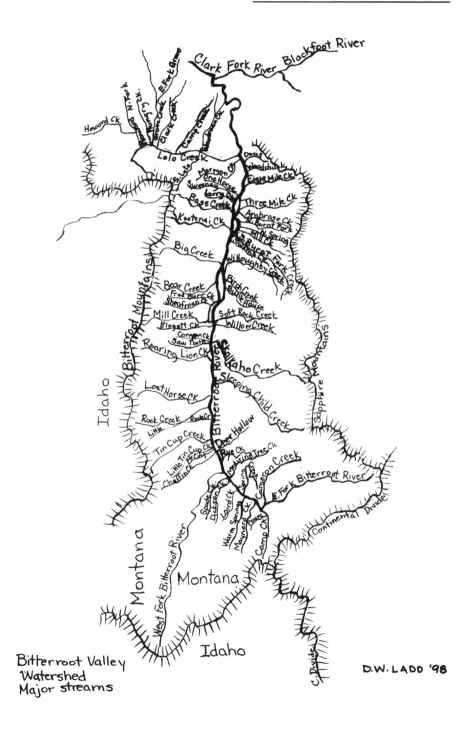

Bitterroot Valley
Watershed
Major streams

D.W. LADD '98

sources indicate the Salish Indians named the river for the red willow (red osier dogwood).

As the Corps proceeded down the valley on the west side of the river they passed through the area where the present-day town of Darby is now located, crossed several creeks, i.e., presently named McCoy, Tin Cup, Rock Creek and Lost Horse. Old Toby persuaded the captains to cross over to the east side of the river which offered easier traveling and better forage for the horses. Soon the valley started to open up. The journalists noted bottoms narrow with timber; large pine and cottonwood. Joseph Whitehouse records, *"valley getting wider, smooth day...soil indifferent. "[6]* Captain Clark also noted that there were no fish. Darkness had fallen before a suitable campsite was found on the east bank of the river southeast of present day Grantsdale, one mile south of Sleeping Child Creek. The hunters brought in two deer, a goose, a crane, a pheasant, and a hawk, which Joseph Whitehouse claimed revived them. *"Our party seemed revived at the success that the hunters had met with, however in all the hardship that they had yet undergone they never once complained, trusting to Providence the Conduct of our Officers in all our difficulties. "[7]*

Darby which was named after the first postmaster who requested the name, "Harrison", which was already assigned. The postmaster, Mr. Darby, received notice that the town would be named "Darby." The community grew around the lumber mills and still is a lumber community approaching a population of nine-hundred.

Grantsdale was surveyed and plotted in June, 1885, at the request of Henry Hamilton Grant who named it Grantsdale. It is now annexed to Hamilton and is a residential community.

The Corps had made it through the first encounter with the awesome Bitterroots and were now well aware of the range to their left. The journals read:

• *"Snow top mountains to our left, "* Clark.[8]

• *"Some of the highest are covered thick with snow, "* Whitehouse.[9]

• *"the snow lays thick on the mountains, a little to our left. "* Whitehouse.[10]

• *"the high snow-topped mountains are still in view to our left."* Patrick Gass.[11]

• *"The snow continues on the Mont. Each side of this valley...Mountains of snow back on our left."* John Ordway.[12]

The travelers hastened through the valley, anxious to start over the final mountain passage to the Columbia River. What were their thoughts? These were not timid men, but their struggle down into the valley over the first range of the Bitterroots was just a prelude to what they knew was coming! Since they had left Fort Mandan on the Missouri River in present-day North Dakota there was no means of communicating with the outside world. They were on their own, at the mercy of the Indians and the elements. The weather had not been friendly. Should they perish over the mountains, no one would ever know about them. Except for Sgt. Floyd's death no one had been lost nor even seriously injured. Would their luck hold? The journals give no indication of such thoughts.

An intriguing route took the Expedition away from the East Fork of the Bitterroot River downstream from Ross' Hole, in September of 1805, because a large rock later known as Jim Hell Rock blocked easy passage along the stream. Spring Gulch brought the travelers back to the stream. The Expedition used this same route in reverse on its return trip in 1806.

Clouds covered the sun on the morning of September 8, 1805. Clark noted that they set out early. The snow-topped mountains on the left reached down to the creek banks. Traveling was not difficult through the valley which opened up to four or five miles wide. They passed present day Skalkaho Creek, Gird, Willow Creek, Soft Rock, Birch, Spoon, and Willoughby.

"Skalkaho" is a Salish word meaning "beaver". It also may mean "many trails." Major Peter Ronan, respected Indian Agent to the Salish in the late 1800's, reported that these Indians "had a curious tradition with respect to beavers. They firmly believed that these animals were a fallen race of Indians, who, in consequence of their wickedness, vexed the Good Spirit, and were condemned by him to their present shape: but that in due time they will be restored to their speech, and that they have heard them talk with each other, and seen them sitting in council on an offending member." Could the future demise of the beaver have been a prelude to what would later be the fate of the Indians?[13]

Along their journey northward the Corps passed over the lands later owned by Marcus Daly on which he developed his famous stock farm and racing horses.

As soon as they got to the Bitterroot Valley, the travelers encountered, as they had on the plains of Montana, the troublesome prickly pear. Its sharp spines easily penetrated the mocassins they wore. (Photo by Pat Hastings)

Near present day Corvallis, probably on the banks of Willow Creek, the Corps lunched on this day and delayed two hours to let the horses graze. They continued their trek down the east side of the river close to where the Eastside Highway now runs. Willow Creek has been the victim of irrigation, and as Dr. Swanzey tells us in *HiLites*, "Willow Creek has been moved around at the whim of a backhoe and allegedly runs like a ditch alongside the Woodside Crossing. Its distinguishing characteristic now is that there is less water in it than in irrigation ditches in the vicinity, and it behaves itself."[14] A rather sad ending to a once wild and free flowing creek.

Corvallis, French for "Heart of the Valley," attracted settlers about 1862 and is a center for the surrounding agricultural area.

A cold wind and a hard rain chilled the travelers. *"We are all cold and wet,"* wrote Clark, *"on this part of the river on the head of Clarks River I observe great quantities of a peculiar Sort of Prickly peare* (observed by Lewis on Aug. 13, 1805) *ovel & about the size of a Pigions egge with throns which is so birded (bearded) as to draw the Pear from the Cluster after penetrating our feet."*[15] At one point in the journey York could not walk from the ravages of prickly pear, Clark's feet were infected and very painful and Lewis described his poor Newfoundland dog, Seaman, as being racked in pain from the bruises and wounds on the pads of his feet.

The land was and is stoney, and the moccasins worn by the travelers gave little protection against bruising, stumbling, and turned ankles. *"Bottoms as also the hills Stoney bad land,"*[16] Clark wrote. Anyone who has farmed or gardened in this valley can attest to Clark's description. The stones are part of the land and enemy to the plow and the shovel. On that day, however, the Corps made twenty-five miles and camped again on the east side of the river in a field one to two miles south of present day Stevensville. Whitehouse described the field as having *"fine feed"* for their horses, and where they were cheered by the hunters' catch that day, an elk and a buck. Now, almost two centuries later, farms and ranches with accompanying homes and outbuildings are scattered over the hills, along with residential rural homes. In the last decade the Stevensville area has become one of the fastest growing regions in Montana.

Stevensville claims to be the first settlement in Montana. In 1841 Father Pierre Jean DeSmet, S.J. founded St. Mary Mission which grew into an Indian village. Here the Jesuit Fathers were responsible for establishing Montana's first church, school, waterwheel, sawmill, orchard, irrigation system, drugstore, agriculture, and cattle ranching. When the priests sold the mission to Major John Owen in 1850, it was the first legal conveyance of property in the Northwest. Major Owen developed Fort Owen as a trading post, never a military post, in the area for trappers, Indians, and white settlers. Major Owen also established a library. Stevensville had its roots.

In 1863 traders Winslett and Houk arrived with pack horses and mules loaded with goods to exchange for hides and furs. About a mile south of Fort Owen they erected the first store. There followed a second store, a saloon, a blacksmith. On May 12, 1864, the few settlers there named the little community "Stevensville" in honor of Isaac Ingalls Stevens, first governor of Washington Territory. President Abraham Lincoln officially proclaimed it so in 1865.

The contact between the Salish Indians and the Lewis and Clark Expedition is salient to an event that occurred in 1831 in St. Louis, Missouri, where Captain Clark was then governor. The Salish and Nez Perce Indians had heard of the "blackrobes", Catholic missionaries, from the Iroquois Indians who came to their valley. The Salish and Nez Perce resolved to get blackrobes themselves to teach religious ways to the people.

A delegation was sent to St. Louis in 1831 to make the request of the Bishop there. After a thousand mile trek through enemy territory and after having suffered many privations, four of the Indians arrived at the home of William Clark. He received them with warm hospitality and interest. However, two of the Indians sickened and died at Clark's home. Their baptism and internment is recorded at the Cathedral in St. Louis: Narcisse, Oct. 31 1831: Paul, Nov. 17, 1831.[17]

Captain Clark's journal for September 9, 1805, mentions only *"a fair morning proceeded on thro a plain as yeterday down the valley. Crossed a large Scattering Creek...a Small one at 10 miles both from the right the main river at 15 miles. Encamped on a large creek from the left which we call Travellers rest Creek."[18]* He then adds, *"killed 4 deer and 4 ducks and 3 prarie fowls."* This is rather a terse entry indicating Captain Clark's urgency to pass through the valley and turn west on the way to the Pacific.

Dr. Swanzey states that the Corps followed the present Eastside Highway fairly closely, and they probably trudged right down the main street of Stevensville. This area was a favorite Indian camp and dance ground, which is why the Jesuits and Major Owen established their mission and fort respectively there. However, the Indians had gone hunting, so there was no reason for the Corps to stop.

On the east bank of the Bitterroot River about a mile north of Stevensville is the Lee Metcalf National Wildlife Refuge, named after the late Senator Lee Metcalf of Montana, a dedicated conservationist whose home was Stevensville. The Refuge, established in 1963, encompasses 2,800 acres of wildlife habitat. It is watered by stream flow and both cold and warm groundwater which is contained in ponds and sloughs designed to attract wildlife. While traveling along the Missouri Lewis and Clark noted

Probable campsite of September 8, 1805, just south of present-day Stevensville, on the east side of the Bitterrroot River. Photo taken in 1998 on that same date. (Photo by Jean O'Neill)

a strange phenomenon which occurs in only a few areas of the West. Canada geese take possession of the empty osprey nests early in the spring. When the osprey return in April and attempt to reclaim their nests, the geese fight them off until the goslings hatch and are old enough to jump or to be pushed from the nests, about a sixty foot drop. Since osprey have been introduced into the Refuge this same phenomenon occurs here.

The travelers proceeded on down the valley and lunched at a spot about a mile east of where the Highway turns west toward Florence. After journeying along four more miles, they crossed the river which Lewis describes as *"it is hear a handsome stream about 100 yards wide and affords a considerable quantity of very clear water, the banks are low and its bed entirely gravel."* Lewis notes also that there are no salmon in the river and concludes that it must have a *"considerable fall in it below"*[19] There is no other mention of fish in the Bitterroot River. Why?

Lewis also reported that Old Toby could not tell them whether or

The Bitterroot River, looking northward, just to the west and north of Stevensville. (Photo by Jean O'Neill)

COLOR SECTION

*(***Editor's Note*** — This section of "Lewis and Clark in The Bitterroot" is intended to give an overview, via paintings and photographs, of both the historical and natural perspectives of the Expedition's stay in the Bitterroot. We are indebted to both the artists and the photographers for their work.)*

THE BITTERROOT FLOWER. *This delicately beautiful flower gave its name to both the Bitterroot Valley and the incredible mountain range to the valley's west side. The bitterroot is the Montana state flower and it also was a major source of food for the Salish Indians who claimed the Bitterroot as their homeland. (Photo by Dale A. Burk)*

ALONG THE TRAIL: LEWIS' WOODPECKER, *by Joe Thornbrugh of Victor, Montana. 18"x15" acrylic on ragboard. Painted especially for this publication. This woodpecker was first described by Meriwether Lewis in the Bitterroot.*

CLARK'S NUTCRACKER, *by Elmer Sprunger of Bigfork, Montana. 8"x10" oil on canvas, painted especially for this publication. The party noted seeing a number of these beautiful high country birds, whose namesake was Captain William Clark. It also was first described in the Bitterroot.*

THE IMPOSING BITTERROOT MOUNTAINS. *These "awesome" and "fearsome" mountains had snow most of the way down them when the Expedition made its way through them, on both the outbound and return trips, but this contemporary view gives a sense of the range's rugged and extensive grandeur. (Photo by Dale A. Burk)*

PONDEROSA PINE NEAR ROSS' HOLE. *Expedition members viewed and wrote about, in their journals, a number of "scarred" trees like this from which the Indians had stripped sections of the tree's cambium layer, mostly for use as food but also for other purposes. Now officially called "culturally scarred trees," they are favorite subjects for photographs along the route of the Expedition through the Bitterroot, particularly at the Medicine Tree Campground along the headwaters of Camp Creek, south of Sula. (Photo by Pat Hastings)*

THE WAPITI (ELK). *This beautiful animal was a major food source for the party while in both the plains and mountain parts of Montana, including the Bitterroot. Here a cow and calf elk are shown in evening light in a photo from Mike Lapinski's stunning full-color book on the American elk titled "The Elk Mystique." Photo courtesy Mike Lapinski.*

LEWIS AND CLARK MEETING THE INDIANS AT ROSS' HOLE, by Charles M. Russell. Mural at Montana State Capitol, 1912. Our cover photograph, this painting is considered by many to be Russell's masterpiece. It depicts the historic encounter between the Expedition and the Oot-la-shoot (Salish) Indians in the upper Bitterroot just after the exhausted party had come over the Bitterroot Mountains from the Lemhi in present-day Idaho.

AT LEMHI, *by Robert F. Morgan of Helena, Montana. Oil on canvas, 1988. This scene depicts the vanguard of the Expedition at the Continental Divide between the Beaverhead River drainage (present-day Montana) and that of the Lemhi River (present-day Idaho). This, literally, was the crown of the continent for the Expedition. (Courtesy Montana State Historical Society.)*

LEWIS AND CLARK'S CAMP AT TRAVELLER'S REST, *by Edgar S. Paxson. Mural at the Missoula County, Montana, Courthouse. This painting represents the Expedition's first encampment to Traveler's Rest along Lolo Creek (in present-day Lolo, Montana) in September of 1805. Droulliard, the hunter, is presenting to Captain Lewis three Salish Indians, whom he discovered while hunting up the creek. Captain Lewis is conversing with Sacajawea, who is sitting beside her husband, Toussaint Charbonneau, and holding her son Pomp. York, the Negro slave, is on the right. Private John Colter leads a stray horse and Private George Shannon leans on his rifle. Seaman, Captain Meriwether Lewis' Newfoundland Retriever dog, is also shown. (Courtesy the Missoula County Board of Commissioners.)*

LEWIS AND CLARK IN THE BITTERROOTS, *by John Clymer. 1967. This famous depiction of the Expedition's incredibly difficult travels through the Bitterroot Mountains has often been called "The Ordeal of the Bitterroots." Sergeant Patrick Gass referred to the Bitterroot Range as "the most terrible mountains I ever beheld." (Courtesy the Clymer Museum of Art)*

THE SALT MAKERS, *by John Clymer. Here the Corps of Discovery makes salt on the shores of the Pacific Ocean, which they hauled back to their winter encampment of 1805-06 at Fort Clatsop in present-day Oregon. (Courtesy the Clymer Museum of Art)*

THE LEWIS CROSSING, by John Clymer. Captain Meriwether Lewis and men are shown crossing the runoff-swollen Clark River (today's Clark Fork River) just below its confluence with the Bitterroot River, in July of 1806 on the party's return journey. (Courtesy the Clymer Museum of Art)

CROSSING THE CLARK'S FORK RIVER, by Edgar S. Paxson. Mural at the Missoula County, Montana, Courthouse. Captain Meriwether Lewis, Sergeant Patrick Gass, John Droulliard, Reuben Fields, Joseph Fields, William Werner, Robert Frazier, Hugh McNeal, John Thompson and Silas Goodrich are shown crossing the Clark Fork River about two and one-half miles below the mouth of the Bitterroot, on July 3, 1806. Captain Lewis is standing at the foot of the tree on the river bank, Droulliard is arranging the packs, and Sergeant Gass stands on shore with the axe. (Courtesy the Missoula County Board of Commissioners)

AT THE HELL'S GATE — JULY 4 1806, *by Robert F. Morgan of Helena, Montana. Oil on canvas, 1994. This scene depicts the party under Captain Lewis' command on the Fourth of July, 1806, leaving their overnight camp on the west bank of Rattlesnake Creek and heading out into the deep canyon on the Clark's Fork River that came to be known as the Hell's Gate. This is one of a number of historic depictions of the Expedition, in both oil on canvas and mural form, by Morgan, who is recognized as a leading authority on the Expedition and whose interpretations of the grand event adorn several major museums in Montana and elsewhere. (Courtesy Montana State Historical Society)*

WILDLIFE. *The Expedition both saw and utilized a variety of wildlife species for sustenance, but these two species were critical factors in providing their supply of food in the Bitterroot — the Franklin grouse, called "fessants" in the journals, (top) and the mule deer. Paintings are by wildlife artist Elmer Sprunger of Bigfork, Montana.*

DINING IN THE BITTERROOT. *A native Bitterroot Valley artist noted for his historical scenes, the late Sandy Ingersoll of Stevensville, Montana, painted this oil, in 1983, of Expedition members at the site of an encampment just outside of where the present town of Stevensville is located.*

not the river flowed into the Columbia, but that to the north it joined another river (today's Clark Fork) that flowed from the east, then *"A man might pass to the missouri from hence by that rout in four days."*[20] It took the Corps fifty-three days to travel here from the Gates of the Mountains. What was Lewis' reaction? He did not record it, although the Hidatsas had told them of the route. Did they not recognize this route as they proceeded up the Missouri? Or were they following President Jefferson's instructions to follow the Missouri to its source? Yet this route would also have required horses, and the Corps had no horses and no means of getting them at that point in the journey.

After trekking five more miles north through a wooded area, the party encamped on a large creek which they named "Travellers Rest", described by Lewis as *"about 20 yards wide a fine bold clear running stream."*[21]

This creek is now called Lolo Creek, probably named after a French trapper, Laurence, who lived and died in this area. The

Another view of the probable September 8, 1805, campsite directly west of the Eastside Highway and just south of the town of Stevensville. (Photo by Jean O'Neill)

Indians had difficulty pronouncing the "r" in Laurence, and Laurence evolved into "Lolo."

The exact location of the Corps encampment on September 9, 1805, is still being investigated. Whitehouse described it, *"We came about 20 miles this day & encamped on a plain near a Creek which run into the River about 2 miles below where we were encamped."*[22] Would there be any artifacts to indicate the exact location? Probably not. Not one item carried by the Corps member was dispensable. If a Corpsman should be so careless as to neglect a tool, knife, gun, pan, weapon, etc., on the trail, he was detailed back to find it. Rarely was anything left behind by this well-disciplined group.

Traveller's Rest Today

The exact location of Traveller's Rest has recently been pinpointed by experts in locating the campsites of the Lewis and Clark Expedition. One of these experts, Dr. Robert T. Bergantino, hydrogeologist at the Montana Bureau of Mines and Technology, at Butte, Montana, has spent the last twenty-five years constructing maps and locating the campsites of the Corps of Discovery on the journey west to the Pacific Coast and on the return. Dr. Bergantino reminds us that the Corps left no markers, so the location of the various campsites is not absolute, but is as close as can be ascertained from the descriptions in the journal — and after nearly two hundred years have passed.

According to the journals, the coordinates of latitude and longitude recorded by the Expedition and also by Clark's map indicate that the site of Traveller's Rest was on the south bank of Lolo Creek about a mile and a half upstream from where the creek empties into the Bitterroot River. This location matches the property owned by Ernie and Pat Deschamps. Recent infrared aerial photographs taken for the Traveller's Rest Chapter of the Lewis and Clark Trail Heritage Foundation, show tepee rings on the bench to the south, which are proof of an historic Indian campsite there, though not necessarily proof of the Expeditions two stops at the site. Lolo Creek has diverted to the north of where it probably was in 1805-1806, but the creek bed and banks are still visible.

Fortunately, the Deschamps have not disturbed the land and have used it only for horse pasture. The creek bed and banks are there to see. Traveller's Rest is largely undisturbed and easily accessible at Lolo, Montana, in the Bitterroot Valley.

CHAPTER SEVEN

DINING IN THE BITTERROOT

"**A**BOUT 11 O'CLOCK *a.m., we halted to dine at a branch"*,[1] states Joseph Whitehouse as the Expedition came into the present-day Stevensville area. Whether food was abundant or meager, midday throughout the journey the travelers would stop to "dine".

Well before the Corps of Discovery put sail up the Missouri, Meriwether Lewis made extensive plans to amass the necessary supplies for the Expedition; among these preparations, he addressed the Corp's dietary needs. The basic idea would be to take along sufficient staples for the journey, but also plan to "live off the bounty of the land" as much as possible. Therefore, he purchased food stuffs to be packed and stored in the keelboat and pirogues. Additionally, there were the tools for food preparation and also for hunting the game they would eat.

Armed with an authorization from President Jefferson, Lewis would buy whatever he might need and charge it to the Army. His list of purchases included these principal foodstuffs: ground corn, 5,555 rations of flour, biscuits, 3 bushel barrels of salt, 4,000 rations of salt pork in kegs, kegs of hogs lard, 600 pounds of "Grees" (lard)[2] and 193 pounds of "Portable Soup" which was a dried soup, an army ration that Lewis may have used during his travels as an Army Paymaster. In those days this soup was used by the armed forces in this and other countries. Lewis enthusiastically had said, that the Portable Soup formed one of the most essential articles in the preparation (for the Expedition). He had the soup prepared for him by Francois Ballet, a cook at 21 North Ninth Street in Philadelphia, who presented a bill on May 30, 1803, for 193 pounds of Portable Soup in the amount of $289.50. This soup was put in 32 tin canisters and "may have been either a dry powder or a thick liquid substance"[3]. There is no known record of its exact composition, but since Lewis put it in canisters one would presume it was a paste or fluid substance. The proportion in cooking preparation would be 1 Tablespoon to each pint of water.[4] Being such a most reliable and nourishing food, it actually contributed to the success of the Expedition itself, as it was used when no other food was available on the trail.

How was this soup paste made? Cutbush describes the preparation of a portable soup or "Tablettes de buillon" in the 1700s. Take calves' feet, 4; the lean part of a rump of beef 12 pounds; fillet of veal 3 pounds; leg of mutton 10 pounds. These are to be boiled in a sufficient quantity of water and the scum taken off. When the meat becomes very tender, the liquor is to be separated from it by expression; and when cold, the fat must be carefully taken off. The jelly-like substance must then be dissolved over the fire and clarified with five or six whites of eggs. It is then to be salted to the taste and boiled down to the consistency of paste, when it is to be poured out on a marble table and cut into pieces, either round or square, and dried in a stove room. Then perfectly hard, they should be put up in close vessels of tine or glass. Powdered rice, beans, peas, barley, celery, with any grateful aromatic may be added".[5]

Supplies purchased by Lewis for campfire meal preparation and also food gathering included: a copper kettle, 14 brass kettles, 1 black tin saucepan, 3 dozen pint tumblers, 30 steels for striking or making a fire, 1 corn mill, 24 iron spoons, and 25 falling axes (fire-wood cutting and many other uses). Hunting and fishing supplies included: 4 "Groce" (gross) fishing hooks — assorted, fish gigs, 44 drawing knives, short and strong, 3 dozen tomahawks, 200 pounds rifle powder, 400 pounds of lead, lead canisters for the gun powder, 15 muzzle loading flintlock long barreled rifles — sometimes called Kentucky rifles, but more properly Pennsylvania rifles, and also additional rifles.[6] On the rifles depended the wild game supply, or in case of an emergency, for self defense.

A list of goods were also included to use as trade items with the Indians who would be encountered along the way. On many an occasion items were traded for food. Sometimes these foods augmented the Corps' supplies, other times the food staved off hunger when the party had no more provisions; they traded for foods like corn, roots, bread, fish, squash, beans, and other vegetables. A few of the items taken on the Expedition for trading (and also for use as gifts) were: 8 brass kettles, 2 corn mills and various metal tools.[7] An example of such trade occurred in February of 1805 while the group was still at the Mandan Indian village. They had run out of meat, but the problem was overcome by trading items made by one of the men, Private John Shields, the Corps' skilled blacksmith. He mended iron hoes, sharpened axes and repaired firearms in exchange for corn. Especially highly prized was a particularly shaped battle axe he made for them. He could scarcely keep up with the demand. Then Lewis and Shields cut up what was left of the stove into pieces of four-inch squares which could then be worked into arrow points or buffalo-hide scrapers. After some haggling, a price was set: seven to eight gallons of corn for each piece of metal."[8]

The Expedition's kettles played a critical part in the journey's success. Not only were they used in general meal preparations and for Indian gifts, they were essential in the making of salt while the Corps spent the winter at Fort Clatsop in what is now western Oregon. Seawater was boiled down in five of the largest kettles. Then the mineral residue would be scraped from the kettles' inside edges. Making salt was a tedious job; boiling was done day and night. This salt would be for the return journey. (Please see color section for depiction of this task by artist John Clymer.)

Kettles were also used in trade for horses from the Indians. During the return trip along the Columbia River, the Captains were in need of acquiring horses. Several times during the month of April, 1806, kettles were used for this trade. On April 19th Clark writes, *"we were oblige to dispense with two of our kittles in order to acquire two of the horses purchased to day. we have now only one Small kittle to a mess of 8 men".*[9] That meant only four kettles left. On the 28th of April Lewis writes about an Indian chief who *"brought a very elegant white horse to our camp and presented him to Captain Clark signifying his wish to get a kettle but on being informed that we already disposed of every kettle we could possibly spear he said he was content with whatever he thought proper to give him".*[10] Capt. Clark gave him his sword, a hundred balls and powder and some small articles with which he appeared perfectly satisfied.

Early in the Expedition Lewis divided the party into three squads, or "messes", which among other things would cook and eat together. Each evening upon landing, Sergeant Ordway would hand out to each mess a day's provisions. It would be cooked at once and a portion reserved for the following day. No cooking was done during the day. Ordway gave out rations in a prescribed order, salt-pork and flour one day, cornmeal and pork the next, and hominy and lard (grease) the next. No pork was issued when freshly killed wild meat was available. To provide game, Drouillard and two or three companions would ride out each day on horses to hunt. Throughout the expedition Drouillard proved to be the best hunter. As Lewis wrote on January 12, 1806, *"I scarcely know how we should subsist it not for the exertions of this excellent hunter."*[11]

The Great Plains of North America, like a real Garden of Eden, provided a great abundance of wildlife. It was a paradise of deer, elk, buffalo, sheep, pronghorns, beaver, coyote, fox, wolves etc. Along the Missouri River Lewis exclaimed, *"We saw immence herds of buffaloe Elk deer & Antelopes.... altho game is very abundant and gentle, we only kill as much as is necessary for food".*[12] Prior to reaching the Rocky Mountains *"the 32 men and one woman would eat every 24 hours: 4 deer or 1 elk and 1 deer, or one buffalo"*[13] which equals to about nine to ten pounds of meat per person, along with some cornmeal and whatever fruit the area afforded. Sometimes the extra meat would be dried or jerked for future eating.

Wild "fruits" of the land were much appreciated. One day in May, 1805, Drouillard and Sacajawea went walking, and she found some wild licorice and dug up a quantity of roots called white apple. Lewis claimed the root was a very healthy food. Lewis realized that a diet of all meat, if not complimented by vegetables and fruits, might lead to scurvy; and there are some indications that the men of the expedition at various times did suffer from scurvy. At other times Sacagawea was able to provide currants, fennel roots and onions she had foraged along the trail.[14]

By the time the Corps of Discovery neared the Lemhi Pass game was getting scarce and supplies were nearly depleted. Lewis woke on the morning of Thursday August 15th, 1805, *"as hungry as a wolf. I had eat nothing yesterday one scant meal of the flour and berries except the dryed cakes of berries which did not appear to satisy my appetite as they appeared to do those of my Indian friends. I found on enquiry of McNeal that we had only about two pounds of flour remaining. this I directed him to divide into two equal parts and to cook the one half this morning in a kind of pudding with burries as he had done yesterday and reserve the ballance for the evening on this new fashioned pudding four of us breakfasted".*[15] The next day Drouillard had killed a deer. All the men were ravenous. The hungry Shoshone Indians with them ate their portions raw. Then Drouillard killed two more deer and Shields killed a pronghorn. The problem of food was solved for that day, at least.

Food supplies were now reduced to a little "pearched corn" and a few tins of portable soup. The Shoshone Indians in the Salmon River Valley were existing on salmon and roots. Since no buffalo lived west of the mountains, they were required to make annual treks to the plains for buffalo hunting. Availability of food was a great concern for all. (As a special note with reference to "pearched corn", it is actually parched corn. Sources indicate that folks over the years claim to a variety of ways to make and use it. Here is one way. This corn is made by the following process: "take fresh green corn, shuck, remove silks and dip the ears in boiling, salted water. Shave off the kernels, getting as little of the cob as possible. Sprinkle the kernels on a cheesecloth pulled tight over a frame, and dry in the sun. When perfectly flaky, press flat with a rolling pin and pack in cloth sacks. Hang in a well-ventilated place. Pioneers hung it by wires from the rafters. To eat the parched corn, soak it in water till soft, heat, and add seasoning to taste.)"[16]

So this was the situation of the Corps of Discovery as they were coming over the mountain pass into a valley, now known as the Bitterroot Valley. Two days before arriving at the campsite we now call Ross' Hole, Ordway wrote in his journal, *"nothing killed this day by the hunters only a fiew fessants. no game of any kind to be Seen in these mountains".*[17] (As a note of interest, "fessents" is probably meant to mean "Pheasants". However, the birds the hunters killed were grouse. Pheasants are not native of Montana, having been imported from Asia into Montana in the early 1880s, well after the Expedition.) The next day only 3 "pheasants" had been killed. Gass and Ordway both attest to eating the last of their pork. Several of the men threatened to kill a colt to eat because they were so hungry.

Let us do a daily itinerary as the Corps trekked up the (Bitterroot) valley struggling to meet its dietary needs. On September 4, 1805, the day of arrival into the valley, the party began the day with only a few grains of parched corn. Then the hunters brought in twelve pheasants and "1 fine deer" to their great joy. Upon this they dined. This was the day they met the friendly band of Salish Indians at Ross' Hole. They had no meat themselves but, as Ordway explains, *"the Indians gave us a pleanty Such as they had to eat, which was only Servis berrys and cherries pounded and dried in Small cakes. Some roots of different kinds."[18]*

The party stayed in camp at Ross' Hole two days. It was not only they that were experiencing hunger. So were the Indians AND their dogs. Patrick Gass tells of the Indian dogs being so hungry that they eat four or five pair of the men's moccasins! Towards the evening of the 5th the hunters killed a deer.

On Friday, the 6th, the Expedition was again on the move. At 1 p.m. they headed north. The Indians, too, were leaving, heading

D.W. LADD '98

A crane (written as "crain" in the journals) was among the wildlife taken by the party for food in September of 1805 in the Bitterroot Valley at their overnight camp near present-day Grantsdale.

east over the mountains to the Missouri River to hunt buffalo. After a seven mile hike (around a mountain now called Sula Peak and down a ravine, Spring Gulch) to a campsite probably near present-day Warm Springs Creek, Clark reports *"this evening nothing to eate but berries our flour out, and but little corn, the hunters killed 2 pheasants only. "[19]* These were critical times for an expedition on the move.

On Saturday the hunters were a little more successful. They killed 2 deer, 1 goose, a crain, several "fessants", and a hawk. Camp that night was in the proximity of present day Grantsdale. This was a substantial improvement from the day before. And on Sunday the 8th, the hunters killed one elk and 1 deer, and Clark killed a "prairie fowl"; the campsite was in today's Stevensville area.

On Monday Lewis reports, *"at 12 we halted on a small branch which falls in to the river on the E. side where we breakfased on a scant portion of meat which we reserved from the hunt of yesterday added to three geese which one of our hunters killed this morning. "[20]* The party arrived on this day at a camp they called Traveller's Rest. The hunters are quite successful but accounts vary a bit. Clark wrote that the hunters brought in 4 deer, 4 ducks and 3 prairie fowls. Ordway records 3 deer, several ducks and 4 pheasants. Either way, Gass writes, we *"have plenty of provisions"*.

September 10, 1805, was also spent at the same campsite. On this day the hunters went out in all directions attempting to get enough meat sufficient to last them in crossing the mountains, because a guide reported that no game would be found on the intended mountainous route. They brought in 4 deer, a faun, a beaver, 3 grouse and 2 ducks, surely not enough food to last very long.

On the 11th all the horses could not be located right away so departure from the camp was delayed. They dined there at noon and finally set out up the creek at 4 p.m. No game was killed this day.

Patrick Gass writes that the "road" was pretty good on the 12th, as it was much traveled by the natives; and they went twenty-three miles. The campsite that night was two miles east of the hot springs. On this day the hunters killed 4 deer and one pheasant. They passed by the springs (Lolo Hot Springs) on Friday the 13th. On this day game was scarce. Captain Clark killed 4 pheasants and Shields killed a Blacktail (Mule) deer.

D.W LADD '98

The camas.

On the morning of the 14th Whitehouse wrote that in the morning they ate the last of their meat. And in *"the eve eat a little Portable Soup but the men in jeneral so hungry that we killed a fine colt which eat verry well, at the time."[21]* The Captains called this place Colt Killed Creek (which is west of Lolo Pass near Powell, Idaho.)

Hunger continued to plague the Corps in the arduous crossing of the mountains. Two days later the Captains ordered a second colt killed, and the next day they ate the third and last colt. Within a month, as they reached the confluence of the Clearwater and Snake Rivers, some of the party were eating dogs which they acquired through trade with the Indians. However, the eating of dog meat was not entirely a result of hunger, but partially in response to choice, as salmon was available at this point in their journey. As Patrick Gass explains on October 9, 1805, *"we have some Frenchmen, who prefer dog flesh to fish, and they here got two or three dogs from the Indians".[22]* Nevertheless, the practice of the Corps eating dogs continued throughout their travels to the Pacific Coast.

During the Expedition's return trip over the Bitterroot Mountains to the (Bitterroot) valley, the availability of game was similar to the fall before; the difference was the ample supply of dried roots which they brought with them. Two days before they arrived at the old campsite at Traveller's Rest, Patrick Gass reported, *"Some hunters went out,*

*as we saw some elk signs here, and our meat is exhausted. We still
have a good stock of roots which we pound and make thick soup of,
that eats very well. In the evening our hunters came in but had not
killed anything. "[23]* The roots were an advantage over their previous
experience here. The next evening they arrived at the warm springs
(Lolo Hot Springs) to camp. Two deer were killed this day. On June
30th, the day of arrival at Traveller's Rest, the hunters had shot five
deer. Surely these hunters were met with enthusiasm from those in
camp. Everyone would eat well that night.

July 1-2, 1806, were spent resting, doing repairs, hunting (over
a dozen deer were shot; abundance, indeed), and making
arrangements for the next leg (actually legs) of their journey.
According to plans laid back at Fort Clatsop, from Traveller's Rest
two groups would separately explore the Marias and the Yellowstone
Rivers.

On the third of July the two groups parted and traveled in
opposite directions, with plans to meet at the Missouri/Yellowstone
junction in five to six weeks. Captain Clark's party went up the west
side of the river, as it was too high at this time to cross over. The
land along the way was tolerably level and partially timbered. They
halted at noon to dine and let their horses feed on a large bottom area
of white clover; then they proceeded on. Many deer were seen on
this day, but only one was killed.

The next day was July 4th. As the party traveled on, they saw
a large band of bighorn sheep. Shots were fired, but all missed their
mark. The date of this day did not go unnoticed by Clark. He writes
in his journal, *"This being the day of the decleration of Independence
of the United States and a Day commonly Scelebrated by my Country
I had every disposition to Selebrate this day and therefore halted
early and partook of a Sumptious Dinner of a fat Saddle of Venison
and Mush of Cows after Dinner we proceeded on... "[24]*

"Cows" is Clark's spelling for "Cous". The dish he cooked was
a porridge/mush he made from bricks of dried Cous roots. These
roots were also known as Kouse, Biscuitroot or Desert Parsley.   The
scientific name is *Lomatium cous* (Wats) and is of the Carrot family,
Umbelliferea.

In the past, this Indian source of food was second in importance
only to camas. Cous grows on dry, open, and rocky places frequently
along with sagebrush, usually in the foothills but sometimes up to

timberline. The range is southeast Washington and northeastern Oregon and east across Idaho to Montana and northwestern Wyoming.[25] This includes the area of the Clearwater and Snake Rivers — home to the Nez Perce tribe. Cous appears in early May and is gathered during most of that month and into June. It is still dug and eaten today. After being gathered, the skin is removed and the root dried. Then the dried roots may be left whole or ground to a powder in mortars and shaped into bricks for future consumption. These cakes or bricks can be dropped into water and made into a mush. It would remind one of Cream of the West roasted hot cereal, but the nutrition content is quite different. There are seventy milligrams of calcium in each cous root. When dried as a "biscuit root" it tasted like a whole wheat cracker — a pleasant nutty flavor.

The method of making cous bricks was to take the ground root powder and moisten it with water and then form it into flat, oblong, square-cornered cakes that were suspended on a framework of flat sticks and partly baked over a slow fire. The bricks were pierced with one or more holes so that they could be strung on a thong and hung from the saddle.

On May 9, 1806, Lewis wrote about this root that the Nez Perce prepared into a most nutritious food. *"cows is a knobbed root of an irregularly rounded form not unlike the Gensang in form and consistance. this root they collect, rub of a thin black rhind which covers it and pounding it expose it in cakes to the sun. these cakes (are) about an inch and 1/4 thick and 6 by 18 in width, when dried they either eat this bread without any further preparation, or boil it and make thick musselage; the latter is most common and much the most agreeable."*[26]

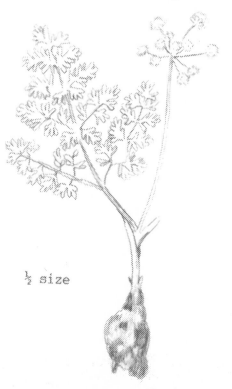

½ size

Illustration by Pat Hastings.

Before the Corps' return crossing over the Bitterroot Mountains, on June 6th, he reported, after trading with the natives, *"on examination we find that our whole party have an ample store of bread and roots for our voyage, a circumstance not unpleasing."*[27]

Let us return to Clark's Fourth of July.

Unfortunately spirits of celebration were probably later dampened, as the party found it necessary to ford several swift running creeks with their horses and got themselves and some of the gear quite wet. Clark notes, *"in crossing this Creek Several articles got wet, the water was So Strong, alto the depth was not much above the horses belly, the water passed over the backs and loads of the horses."*[28]

The next day the travelers crossed the West Fork and many other channels, finally arriving on the east side of the (Bitterroot) river. At the foot of a mountain they stopped to dry out all the wet articles and let the horses graze. Then later in the afternoon they crossed the mountain to the valley where they first camped with the Indians on September 4, 1805, ten months earlier. The hunters killed two deer and one bighorn sheep on this day. This time, while passing through the (Bitterroot) valley, hunger was not such a burden as it had been the previous fall. Game was more plentiful and the party was carrying the root cakes they had obtained from the Nez Perce.

On the 6th day of July, 1806, Clark took his party on the-well traveled Indian route over the Continental Divide (via Gibbons Pass) into the (Big Hole) valley beyond, and on their way toward Camp Fortunate.

In conclusion, halting to "dine" while in the Bitterroot Valley must surely have been focal points in the daily routine of the Expedition; but there was a difference for the Corps of Discovery between the journey westward in 1805, and the return passage in 1806. On the westward trek they dealt with a near constant companion of hunger; game was scarce, meals were meager and vitality was at a low ebb. In contrast, during Clark's return trip nearly a year later, meals were more substantial, and spirits were running higher — even a special meal to celebrate the 4th of July! The feared, snowy Bitterroot Mountains had been crossed for the second time, and the homeward-bound party looked forward to reaching Camp Fortunate, among other things to retrieve the cached tobacco! — and to proceed on to regroup with Lewis and the rest of the Expedition at the mouth of the Yellowstone River.

CHAPTER EIGHT

THE NATURE OF THINGS

ONE OF THE important assignments with which President Thomas Jefferson charged Meriwether Lewis while on the expedition was to collect and describe plant, animal and mineral specimens. As Jefferson said himself of Lewis, he was "an attentive farmer, observing with minute attention all plants and insects he met with."[1] On June 20, 1803, President Jefferson wrote a letter of instructions to Lewis regarding the objectives of the mission. After drafting a long list of observations to be carried out, he states, "Other objects worthy of notice will be:

• the soil & face of the country, its growth & vegetable productions: especially those not in the U.S.

• the animals of the country generally & especially those not known in the U.S. the remains and accounts of any which may be deemed rare or extinct the mineral productions of every kind; but more particularly metals, limestone, pit coal & saltpetre; salines & mineral waters, noting the temperature of the last, & such circumstances as may indicate their character.

• Volcanic appearances.

• climate as characterized by the thermometer, by the proportion of rainy, cloudy & clear days, by lightning, hail, snow, ice, by the access & recess of frost, by the winds prevailing at different seasons, the dates of which particular plants put forth or lose their flowers, or leaf, times of appearances of particular birds, reptiles or insects."[2]

Therefore, in that year of 1803 while Lewis was making extensive arrangements for the Expedition, he also spent time in Philadelphia with Dr. Benjamin Smith Barton, professor of the University of Pennsylvania. Professor Barton was the author of the first textbook about Botany in the United States and he also had studied in England and Germany. Barton was captivated by the Expedition and would have even liked to go, too! Nevertheless, he made his contribution by teaching Lewis how to preserve specimens — plants, birds or animals. Also he instructed him regarding the importance of specimen labeling and place and date of the collection. Instruction included an expanded range of biological knowledge — a list of over two hundred terms for describing new plants and animals. Lewis developed a remarkable awareness of scientific terminology. The Expedition would be a scientific one as well as one that sought a river passageway to the Pacific.

Captain William Clark was also an excellent naturalist. So together Captains Lewis and Clark were to contribute considerably to knowledge of the biological diversity of North America by obtaining and sending back, or bringing back, botanical and zoological specimens for scientific collections. They usually shot or otherwise caught an individual of each species of wildlife and measured and described them; their plant collection still exists at the Philadelphia Academy of Natural Sciences. They saw and were the first to describe many species of animals and plants unknown to science.[3]

Because the journals focused upon careful scientific observation, they are extremely valuable as today we try to understand the real character of nature beyond the Mississippi River before it was altered by the settlement of the West. While the Corps of Discovery passed through what is known today as the Bitterroot Valley, Lewis noted countless plants, birds and animals in his journals. The following will include highlights of a few special examples of these, and the remaining will be listed in their groupings.

Plants

The Bitterroot Valley is named after a little plant that flowers so beautifully in this area in late spring. And the Corps of Discovery is integrally connected with its story. Captain Meriwether Lewis first handled and investigated the root of the bitterroot plant in August of 1805. This was the first known experience of a white man with the plant, but at the time Lewis knew only that the root of it was bitter for his taste and that the Shoshone Indians *"ate them heartily"*.[4]

In his journal of August 22, 1805, the clue to the identification

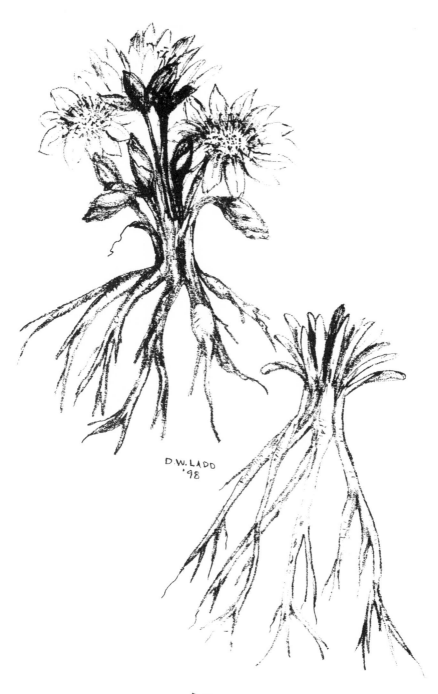

Bitterroot

was the description of the root. *"Another species was much mutulated but appeared to be fibrous; the parts were brittle, hard — the size of a small quill, cilindric and white as snow throughout except some parts of the hard black rind which they (the Indians) had not separated in the preparation. This the Indians with me informed were always boiled for use. I made the experiment, found that they became soft by boiling, but had a very bitter taste. "[5]* Lewis was only able to see the root structure of this plant at this time of the season, since the bitterroot is only in bloom in late spring.

But the next summer as the Expedition returned to the valley and was again camped at Travellers Rest (from June 30 to July 3, 1806), Lewis was awarded the pleasure of seeing the plants' blossoms. And it was during this time that he preserved some plants for his collection. Because we know now how the wild bitterroot plants thrive on dry, well drained, exposed hillsides — often on

Wild rose.

rocky or shallow soil, one would assume that Lewis hiked upon the hills adjacent to the creek to come across the pink and white flowers nestled close to the ground. He did not realize how lucky he was to find them in bloom at this late date (July 2nd), for normally the plants have set seeds by late June. Rarely are they in bloom past mid-June. But it was a late spring in 1806 as indicated by the unusual snow depth in western Montana the previous winter. Clark noted in his records that on June 17, 1806, the snow depth at the Lolo Pass was still six to seven feet deep.[6]

They also found a mountain Lady Slipper in bloom that late June, which is another indication of a late season.

Like the other collected plant material, Lewis collected, pressed and dried his bitterroot plants. These were described as *"other uncommon plant specimens"*.[7] Ultimately he brought this invaluable collection on the 3,000 miles of an incredible route of horse, boat and stagecoach to reach Philadelphia in 1807.

Bernard McMahon, a well known horticulturist and seed merchant in Philadelphia, wrote to Lewis before his arrival. McMahon urged Lewis to consider having the widely respected German-born botanist, Frederick Pursh, look at the collection. Pursh had now been in the United States for eight years.[8]

So, in April of 1807, Lewis delivered his dried collection to McMahon and Pursh. Included, of course, were the bitterroot plants collected while at the Traveller's Rest campsite. As McMahon examined them, he noticed some new growth. And, at a later date, in 1814, he wrote that the planted roots "vegetated for more than a year" — a very tenacious plant indeed.[9] In any event, when Pursh gave the bitterroot plant its scientific name, he called it *Lewisia rediviva* (Pursh). The Genus name is for Captain Lewis, and the "rediviva" refers to McMahon's experience with the plants' amazing ability to revive after being dried for many years. Webster's dictionary says that rediviva means "living again".

This plant is in the Purslane family which is shared with the Western Spring Beauties and the Alpine Spring Beauties. It is a truly beautiful wildflower, which is now scarce in many localities. It is pale pink or even white to deep rose and has about fifteen rounded or pointed overlapping petals. The flower is one and one-half to three inches across. The blossoms appear just above the ground line on short stems that rise directly from a deep root crown. Round in

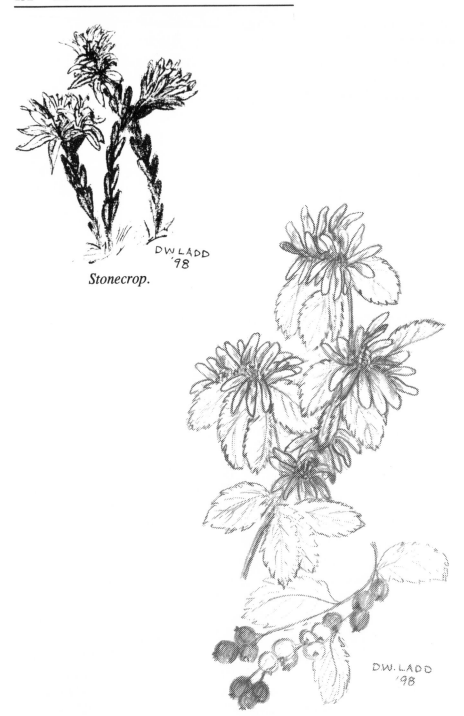

Stonecrop.

Serviceberry.

cross-section and fleshy succulent, the leaves also grow from the root, three-fourths to two inches long. The leaves begin to wither before the flowers emerge in May and June, sometimes giving the impression that the plants have no life-supporting leaves.[10]

Jerry DeSanto, in his book, "Bitterroot," describes the collecting of the plant by natives years ago, a plant they called "spit-lum". "Among the natives of western Montana, the time of bitterroot harvesting was an annual event of great sociability and much significance."[11] In the Bitterroot Valley, the resident Flathead Indians were joined by other Salisan tribes during the "Bitterroot Month", the fifth lunar month of the year. This practice continued until approximately 1933; but sporadic visits continued up to the early 1970s. "Though accounts vary, it seems that the optimum time for gathering bitterroot was in May. The distinctive basal leaves of the plant were then easily recognizable and buds were less bitter then, than later. They also must have known that the roots contained more starch then, than at any other time... bitterroot was valued for starch and not for sugar."[12]

With digging sticks called "pee-cha" they dug "the plant out by trenching the earth about four or five inches from the plant. Lift the earth and pull out the plant, simultaneously, the entire four to six inch root will come out unharmed. Knock the dirt off, back into the hole, top the plant by pulling at the leaves and buds until they separate from the root. Break a section of the red, root skin at the crown of the root and strip it down. Throw the plant, buds and skin back in the hole to grow again."[13] The roots were peeled after digging, washed and then dried in the sun. They were kept dry until use and then steamed for about twenty minutes on a bed of twigs over a boiling kettle. Then the roots were eaten plain, served with meat as a stew or sweetened with berries.

It is a tribute to this precious beauty that our very scenic valley in western Montana is named the Bitterroot Valley. Additionally special is that the Bitterroot flower has become Montana's State flower. Early in the year of 1894 the Montana Legislature announced that it would accept ballots to name a state flower. By September 1st, over 5,000 ballots had been received. Thirty-two different flowers had been suggested. The top three were: the Bitterroot, Evening Primrose, and the Wild Rose. The Bitterroot received 3,621 ballots. Therefore, in the 1895 January session, the Legislature responded to the public and declared the Bitterroot the State Flower.

It is unfortunate that as the years go by and the Bitterroot Valley becomes more developed and populated, there are fewer and fewer of these flowers to bloom. The plants' habitat is gradually and continually being decreased. Some of its choice areas have been taken over as pasture land for stock animals, and housing development takes another big toll.

Other Plants

It is curious that the journals do not mention the occurrence of sagebrush in the valley. But after all, for months the party had been passing through landscapes of sagebrush; so this must have been unremarkable. Nevertheless, early settlers in the Corvallis area were impressed with the tall, dense stands of sagebrush growing in that area. Today varieties of Artemisia thrive on the dry hillsides, especially on the east side of the valley

Other plants which were mentioned in the journals were: *"small head or wooly clover, wild rose, service berry, white berryed honeysuckle, thin lead owlclover, wormleaf stonecrop, wild strawberry, wild vining honeysuckle, gooseberries, Camas, Yellow bells, Purple trillium, Ragged Robin, Mariposa lily, and Mountain Lady's slipper".*[14]

Birds

On August 22, 1805, the expedition was by the Salmon River before coming over the pass from the Idaho side into the (Bitterroot) valley when Capt. Clark wrote, *"I saw today a Bird of the woodpecker kind which fed on Pine burs, its bill and tale white, the wings black, every other part of a light brown, and about the size of a robin."*[15] This bird is now called Clark's Crow or Clark's Nutcracker. Nutcrackers are common in the timbered foothills of the Bitterroot Valley and surely the party saw many nutcrackers as they ascended the pass to Ross' Hole and again as they started up the Lolo trail westward. To see the Clark's Nutcracker today is a nice reminder of Captain Clark and the Expedition's trip through the Rock Mountains. The scientific name of the Clark's Nutcracker is: *Nucifraga columbiana.* This is in the *Family Corvidea*, which includes Crows, Ravens, Magpies and Nutcrackers. The bird is twelve to thirteen inches from beak to tip of its tail and is locally common in conifers near timberline where it nests. It has flashy white wing and tail patches and a gray body. A long sharply pointed bill and a white face confirm its identification at a distance. Additionally, its flight and general body form is crow-like. A drawn out grating Kr-a-a-a is its call.

Again, while still on the other side of the pass, Clark was just below the mouth of the Lemhi River where it runs into the Salmon River when he reported seeing *"some fiew pigions"*.[16] Even though pigeons were not recorded as having been seen in the Bitterroot Valley — but close to it — this species has since become extinct and deserves mentioning. "Thus, it is on record that passenger pigeons were to be found in Idaho, west of the Continental Divide in 1805 and that Clark was the first to report their presence there."[17]

Another most interesting bird which Lewis wrote about was a woodpecker that ultimately was named the Lewis' Woodpecker. Even today, this woodpecker still lives in the Bitterroot Valley, although it is now not commonly seen. Its scientific name is *Melanerpes*

The Clark's Nutcracker.

Canada goose.

Lewis, and it is in the *Family Picidae* which includes Woodpeckers, Flickers and Sapsuckers. While the expedition was toiling through the Montana Rocky Mountain wilderness in 1805, Lewis saw a big, dark woodpecker flying with the rowing wingbeat of a crow. But it wasn't until the next spring that he got a close look. The party was camped with the Nez Perce tribe at Camp Chopunnish in Idaho when on May 27, 1806 — just a month before the expedition came back over Lolo Pass — one of the men brought Lewis a black colored woodpecker which he had previously noted but not held. With a description of 500 words he stated, *"the throat is of a fine crimson red, the belly and breast is a curious mixture of white and blood red"*, *"wings and tail are of a sooty black"*, *"top of the head black... with a glossy tint of green in a certain exposure"*, and so forth.[18] Lewis preserved the skin of this bird. (Again on July 1st, while at Traveller's Rest he mentions a *"black woodpecker"*.) The following spring this bird specimen accompanied Lewis's entire biological collection which was delivered for study. It is interesting to note that today this particular bird skin is at the Harvard University and is the only surviving zoological specimen.[19]

The Lewis' Woodpecker measures from ten and one-half to

eleven and one-half inches long. It is a large black-backed woodpecker with an extensive pinkish red belly (the only North American woodpecker so colored). It has a wide gray collar and a dark red face patch. The pink underparts and wide black wings are the best marks. The sexes are similar. It has a straight crow-like flight.[20] It frequents open stands of pine and scattered trees beside streams... A favorite haunt is the charred remnant of a burned-over forest. This bird eats insects by snapping them up in the air, but also eats freely on the ground — ants, grasshoppers, crickets, and beetles. Its voice is usually silent, but occasionally there is a harsh but soft churr or chee-ur. As of the summer of 1997, sightings of the Lewis' Woodpecker include at the Lee Metcalf National Wildlife Refuge near Stevensville and also a nesting pair by the Rye Creek Road south of Darby. (Please turn to the Color Section to view a painting of the Lewis Woodpecker by artist Joe Thornbrugh.)

Lewis noted two other birds of special interest while at Traveller's Rest. First, it was Canada Geese. One day the hunters brought back three geese which they had killed in the morning. It is fascinating to read in the expedition's earlier journals — when they were yet on the way up the Missouri River, Lewis and Clark were the first white men to observe Canada Geese nesting in trees. Subsequently when ornithologists read these reports, they attempted to discredit them. However, later naturalists of this same region (along the Missouri east of Great Falls), Elliot Coues among them, discovered these birds still nesting in trees.[21]

The second bird appeared when *"two of our hunters arrived, one of them brought with him a red headed woodpecker of the large bird common to the United States."*[22] This was surely the Pileated Woodpecker, occasionally seen today along the Bitterroot River and also in the dry forest areas.

Other birds mentioned in the journals were: *"Mourning Dove"*, *"lark"* (Northern Flicker), *"logcock"* (probably Horned Lark), *"Sandhill crain"* (Sandhill Crane), *"prarie hen with the short and pointed tail"* (Sharptailed Grouse), *"robin"* (American Robin), *"a species of brown plover"* (probably Upland Sandpiper), *"curloos"* (Long billed Curlew), *"small black birds"* (Rusty Blackbirds or Brewer's Blackbirds), *"raven"* (Common Raven), *"hawks"*, *"variety of sparrows"*, *"bee martins"* (Western Kingbird)[23], Brown headed Cowbird, and the Western Meadowlark.[24] The Western Meadowlark has since become the Montana State bird. In 1930 Montana's school children were polled to select the bird that most represented their state. The response overwhelmingly favored the Western Meadowlark. The 1931 Legislature agreed with the choice and declared the Western Meadowlark the official bird of Montana.[25]

Insects

With regards to the mention of insects, it was principally the mosquito! At Travellers Rest, Lewis says, *"The musquetoes have been excessively troublesome to us since our arrival at this place."* That same day Clark writes, *"The musquetors has been so troublesome day and night since our arrival in this Vally that we are tormented very much by them and Can't write except under our Bears."*[26] (*"Bears"* is Clark's spelling for *"bowers"* or mosquito netting.)

Animals

The kinds of animals encountered by the party were also those which were shot for food — even some of the squirrels were eaten. They were: mule deer, whitetailed deer, elk, bighorn sheep — (which were sometimes termed *"Ibex"*), beaver, rabbits (Nuttails cottontail), small grey squirrel (Richardson's red squirrel), and the Columbian ground squirrel. (Also taken for food were some birds: the Sandhill Crane and the Sharptailed Grouse.)

Fish

Little is mentioned regarding fish in the Clark's River (Lewis's name for the Bitterroot River), or its side creeks. Perhaps that was because the group was on horseback and not traveling the riverway, or that time was of the essence to move on so that they didn't do any fishing. The only record Lewis makes is about a species of fish that he DOESN'T see. On September 9, 1805, he describes the Clark's River as being *"about 100 yards wide and affords a considerable quantity of very clear water, the banks are low and its bed entirely gravel. the stream appears navigable but from the circumstances of being no sammon in it I believe that there must be a considerable fall in it below."*[27]

Trees

A number of tree species were included in their writings. Among them were: *"seven bark"*, elder (Common Eldeberry), choke cherry, broad leafed willows (Bebb Willow, Scouler Willow, and Yellow Willow), narrow leafed willows (Sandbar or Coyote willow), fir and larch (which they found in higher parts of the hills and mountains), long leafed pine (Ponderosa Pine), — the principal timber of the neighborhood and grows well in the river bottoms as on hills, lodgepole pine, black cottonwood, alder aspin (Quaking Aspen), and birch.[28]

Landscape

In those early September days of 1805, as the group made its way from south to north through the valley, descriptions of the landscape were recorded to include comments like: the country was mountainous and poor, there were snow topped mountains to the left (Bitterroot Range), and open hilly country on the right. In today's Hamilton area the plain was smooth and dry; the valley was about two miles wide and the lands poor and stony.

Closer to where Stevensville is located today, the bottoms as well as the hills were stony, bad land. The hills on the right-hand (east) were only partially covered with pine but mostly barren. There was some snow on the mountains to the right (Sapphire Range). In today's North Burnt Fork Creek area the valley was described as being generally a prairie of smooth, pleasant plain — from five to six miles wide. The growth was almost entirely pine and some spruce.

Near the water courses they found a small proportion of cottonwood.[29] This was not a countryside with areas of fertile growth, but instead described, in large part, with terms as — *"poor, stoney, and barren"*. How different the valley was to become over time, as irrigation practices changed much of the landscape for farming and ranching — to say nothing of fencing, the development of buildings, roads, bridges, powerlines, signs etc..

Hot Springs

Recalling Jefferson's letter of instructions in 1803, Lewis was to document *"salines and mineral waters, noting the temperature of the last, and such circumstances as may indicate their character"*.

The Corps of Discovery first passed by what is known today as

Cottontail rabbit.

Lolo Hot Springs, as they journeyed into the Bitterroot Mountains on September 13, 1805, Lewis wrote, *"at two miles passed Several Springs ... one of the Indians had made a whole to bathe, I tasted the water and found it hot and not bad tasted ... found this water nearly boiling at the places it Spouted from the rocks which a hard Corse Grit, and of great size the rocks and on the Side of the Mountain of the Same texture. I put my finger in the water, at first could not bare it in a Second."[30]* Patrick Gass described a *"most beautiful warm spring, the water of which is considerably above blood-heat."[31]* A precise temperature reading of the springs was impossible, since Lewis's last thermometer had broken eight days before during the arduous crossing of the Divide. Now, the expedition was bent on getting over the mountains as quickly as possible, so they did not linger at the springs. It wasn't until on their return trip the following June (June 29, 1806) did they take time to appreciate them. Clark describes the event with some detail. *"Those Worm or Hot Springs are Situated at the base of a hill of no considerable hight, on the N side and near the bank of travellers rest Creek (Lolo Creek) which is at the place about 10 yards wide. these Springs issue from the bottom and through the interstices of a grey freestone rock, the rock rises in irregular masy clifts in a circular range, around the Springs on their river Side. imediately about the Springs on the Creek there is a hansom little quamash plain of about 10 acres. the principal Spring is about the temperature of the Warmest baths used at the Hot Springs in Virginia. in this bath which had been prepared by the Indians by stopping the river with Stone and mud, I bathed and remained in 10 minits it was with difficuelty I could remain this long and it caused a profuse swet. two other bold Springs adjacent to this are much warmer, their heat being so great as to make the hand of a person Smart extreemly when immerced ... both the Men and the indians amused themselves with the use of the bath this evening. I observe after the indians remaining in the hot bath as long as they could bear it run and plunge themselves into the Creek the water of which is now as Cold as ice Can make it. after remaining here a fiew minits they return to the worm bath repeeting this transision Several times but always ending with the worm bath."[32]*

As one reflects upon the biological contributions which were made during the Lewis and Clark Expedition that involved the carefully recorded descriptions and observations, the conscientiously compiled collections, and the listing of so many other species, one captures a glimpse into the "nature of things" of the Bitterroot Valley two centuries ago.

LOLO HOT SPRINGS

THE TRAVELERS PASSED HERE WESTBOUND
THE MORNING OF SEPTEMBER 13, 1805.

CLARK WROTE, ... "I tasted this water and found it hot & not bad tasted ... in further examonation I found this water nearly boiling hot at the places it Spouted from the rocks ... I put my finger in the water, at first could not bare it in a Second."

ON THE RETURN JOURNEY THEY CAMPED HERE JUNE 29, 1806 ENJOYING A HOT BATH AND FOUR DEER FOR SUPPER, THEIR FIRST FRESH MEAT IN FIVE DAYS.

CLARK WROTE, ... "I observe after the indians remaining in the hot bath as long as they could bear it run and plunge themselves into the creek the water of which is now as cold as ice can make it." ...

MEDICINE

By the time the Corps of Discovery reached Lemhi Pass they had encountered hardships and diseases few people could withstand. Dysentery, tumors, boils, abscesses, felons, heat exhaustion, bruises and venereal disease are just a few of the health problems they faced. And various other afflictions would trouble them on their journey through the Bitterroot Valley and the rugged Bitterroot Mountains. Captain Meriwether Lewis had learned from his mother at an early age the healing properties of herbs, and before Lewis left Philadelphia, he received guidance from Dr. Benjamin Rush. Dr. Rush gave him a list of medications to take on the journey, as follows:

15 pounds Pulv. Cor. Peru, ½ pound pulverized jalap, ½ pound pulverized Rhei (rhubarb), 4 ounces pulverized Ipecacuan., 2 pounds pulverized Crem. Tart., 2 ounces gum camphor, 1 pound gum assafoetid, ½ pound gum Opii Turk. opt., ¼ pound gum Tragacanth, 6 pounds Sal Glauber, 2 pounds Sal. Nitri, 2 pounds Copperas, 6 ounces Saccar. Saturn. Opt., 4 ounces Calomel, 1 ounce Tartar Emetic, 4 ounces Vitriol Alb., ½ pound Rad. Columbo, ½ pound Elix Vitriol, ¼ pound Ess. Menth. pip., ¼ pound Bals. Copaiboe, ¼ pound Bals. Traumat., 2 ounces Magnesia, ¼ pound Indian Ink, 2 ounces Gum Elastic, 2 ounces Nutmegs, 2 ounces Cloves, 2 ounces Cinnamon, 4 ounces Laudanum, 2 pounds Ung. Basic Flav., 1 pound Ung. (...) Calimin, 1 pound Ung. Epispastric, 1 pound Ung. Mercuriale, 1 Emplast. Diach. S., 1 Set Pocket Insts. small, 1 Set Teeth Insts. small, 1 Clyster Syringe, 4 Penis do., 3 Best Lancets, 1 Tourniquet, 2 ounces Patent Lint, 50 dozen Bilious Pills to Order of B. Rush, 6 Tin Canisters, 3.9 ounces Gd. Stopd. bottles, 5 4-ounce Tinctures do, 6 4-ounce Salt Mo., 1 Walnut Chest, 1 Pine do.

The greatest item on the list is fifteen pounds of Pulv. Cort. Peru at a cost of thirty dollars. Peruvian Bark is now known as Quinine or Cinchona. "Giving the bark" as mentioned in the journals of the expedition refers to the administration of this substance. This drug was used primarily for fever and chills, or "intermittents," a general term for recurring fever, and could be called the aspirin of the day because of its varied use.

An interesting way of treating "intermittents" is discussed in the

1729 volume of *Domestic Medicine or The Family Physician*, by William Buchen, M.D.: "First thing to be done in cure is to cleanse the first passage. This not only renders the application of other medicines more safe but efficaceous. In this disease quantities of bile are discharged by vomit, which plainly points out the necessity of such evacuations. Vomits are therefor to be administered before the patient takes any other medicine. A dose of ipecacoanha will generally answer the purpose very well. (Ipecac is still a staple of Emergency Rooms, used to induce vomiting when some poisons have been ingested.) One-half dram of the powder will be sufficient for an adult, for a younger person must be less in proportion. Purging medicine are likewise useful, and often necessary, in intermitting fevers. A smart purge has been known to cure an obstinate ague, after the Peruvian Bark and other medicines have been used in vain. Vomits, however are more suitable in this disease, and render purging less necessary, but if the patient is afraid to take a vomit, he ought in this case to cleanse the bowels by a dose or two of glauber salts, jalop or rhubarb. Bleeding may sometimes be proper at the beginning of an intermitting fever, when excessive heat, delerium &c. give reason to suspect an inflammation, but as the blood is very seldom in an inflamatory state in intermitting fever, this operation is rarely necessary."

The preceding paragraph is a direct quote from this early self-help book. Since treatment has not changed much in intervening years, one could surmise that Lewis and Clark may have gone by similar guidelines.

Another major item on the medical supply list was fifty dozen Bilious Pills that became know as Rush's Pills and/or Thunderclappers or Rush's Thunderbolts. They were a very potent laxative, nicknamed appropriately because of their fast action.

Dr. Rush gave Lewis the ten health commandments for preserving the health of the men on the expedition, although he could rarely adhere to these rules. They are as follows:

1. Flannel worn next to the skin, especially in winter.

2. Always to take a little raw spirits after being very wet or much fatigued; and as little as possible at any other time.

3. When you feel the least indisposition, fasting and rest; and diluting drinks for a few hours, take a sweat, and if costive take purge of two pills every four hours until they operate freely.

4. Unusual costiveness is often the sign of an approaching disease. When you feel it, take one or two of the opening pills.

5. Where salt cannot be had with your meat, steep it a day or two in common lye.

6. In difficult and laborious enterprises or marches, eating sparingly will enable you to bear them with less fatigue and more safety to your health.

7. Washing feet with spirit when chilled, and every morning with cold water.

8. Molasses or sugar with water with vit. (vituals) and for drink with meals.

9. Shoes without heels.

10. Lying down when fatigued.

Number seven and nine on the list of health commandments refer to the care of feet. The feet of the Corps members were especially traumatized by rough terrain and the spines of the prickly pear cactus. Often these cactus spines remained embedded in their skin and caused infections. Thin-soled moccasins were their only protection and were inadequate. By the light of the evening campfire in July of 1805, Captain Clark removed seventeen cactus spines from his feet.

Wind and dust certainly played a part in the travails that were encountered. Sore eyes may have been caused by these irritants. The people of the Indian Nations along the Columbia drainage had sore eyes and blindness. Lewis or Clark treated their eyes with vitriol, a topical solution of zinc sulfate and lead acetate.[33]

Although there were few incidents of serious injuries, on the return journey both Potts and Lewis had open wounds. On the return journey through the Bitterroot Mountains, on June 18, 1806, Lewis made note of John Potts' injury. *"Potts cut his leg very badly with a knife It bled badly because of a blood vessel laceration"*. Lewis made a tourniquet. Sergeant Ordway wrote, *"Lewis sowed up the wound and bound it up"*. On June 22 Lewis noted, *"Potts legg is inflamed and very painfull to him. We apply poltis of roots and cous"*. Then on June 27 Lewis wrote, *"Potts leg which had been much swelled and inflaimed for several days is much better this evening and give him but little pain. He apply the roots and leaves of wild ginger from which he found great relief."*[34]

Wild ginger could not have been growing at the elevation they were at this time. They may have dug it earlier, found it useful, and carried a supply with them.

When Lewis was accidentally shot by his fellow traveler, Cruzatte, a few clues are given about treatment of open wounds. Lewis dressed the wound himself by "introducing tents of patent lint into the ball holes." Lint is described in the dictionary as linen scraped and made soft, once used to cover wounds. He also had a poultice of Peruvian bark applied to the wound.

Echinacea purpurrea.
(Purple cone flower)

Meriwether Lewis had a continuing interest in the use of herbs and their healing power. Another herb that Lewis found interesting for its use among the Mandan and Hidasta Indians was Echinacia. It is described as a cure for snake bite and mad dog bite, even after the wound from dog bite was scabbed over, although it was recommended the wound be re-opened. At the time of its use among the Indians, the roots and stems were chewed but not swallowed (taking internally was not recommended), the chewed portion then applied to the wound twice daily until healed.[33] Now Echinacea is a widely used herbal remedy taken internally to stimulate the immune system. Its common name is purple cone flower.

Also on the return trip, Silas Goodrich and Hugh McNeal were ill with the "pox" otherwise known as Louis veneri or syphilis. They had been treated at Fort Clatsop, and thought to have been cured. They were treated again at the falls of the Missouri, probably using mercury salve and calomel (mercurous chloride).

The men of the Corps of Discovery had few medicines and resources at their command. Although the venereal diseases which they contracted during the journey continued to plague some of the members throughout their lives, most came through with few ill effects. This is a testament to the men's common sense and ingenuity.

Probable campsite of the Expedition at Traveller's Rest on September 9-10, 1805, located on the property of Ernie and Pat Deschamps, at Lolo, looking west. (Photo by Jean O'Neill)

CHAPTER NINE

TRAVELLER'S REST — 1805

TRAVELLER'S REST IS a name which belies the attitude and activity of the Corps of Discovery on September 9 and 10, 1805. The only ones on the Expedition that really rested were the horses which were let out to graze before starting their arduous trek over this range of the Bitterroot Mountains in Montana and Idaho. But this was a breather for the weary travelers, time to gather their thoughts, contemplate the next step of the journey, and gird themselves psychologically for the rigorous passage ahead of them. Here, Old Toby indicated, they must now turn west. The hunters were sent out to bring in provisions as the Indians had warned the captains that there was little or no game in the mountains. Two of the hunters were directed to return to the river and follow it to its junction with the *"Eastern fork"* (the present-day Clark Fork at Missoula) and report back that evening. One of the hunters (Colter) returned with three Salish (probably Nez Perce) Indians he had encountered up Traveller's Rest Creek and who were pursuing some Indians they claimed were Snake (or Shoshone) who had stolen 23 horses. The three related how they were alarmed at seeing Colter, but he soon calmed their fears when he lay down his gun and advanced toward them. Lewis wrote of them, *the Indians were mounted on very fine horses of which the Flatheads have a great abundance; ...each man in the nation possess from 20 to a hundred head. "[1]* Old Toby could not speak their language, but through sign language, which Lewis claimed was common to all Aborigines of North America, they told their story.

The captains gave them a ring fish hook, some steel, a little powder to make a fire and tied a ribbon in their hair which pleased them. Two of the Indians hastened after the thieves who had stolen their horses, the third offered to remain and guide the white men to his relatives whom he claimed lived on a prairie over the mountains on the Columbia river. And, he indicated the journey would last five sleeps. When the hunters returned they had netted only four deer, a beaver and a grouse.

One of Captain Lewis' main reasons for stopping at Traveller's Rest was to take *"celestial observations,"* which he recorded as Latitude 46 degrees 41' 38.0. The men and Sacajawea had many tasks and busied themselves making moccasins and repairing clothing. Tools needed to be sharpened, guns prepared for the journey. Medicines and food were checked and repacked on the horses.

Perhaps Sacajawea found roots and berries to supplement their meals. Did she croon to her baby as she went about her work? What songs did the men sing as they worked or trudged along the trails? Did Cruzette bring out his fiddle and play a few French tunes when

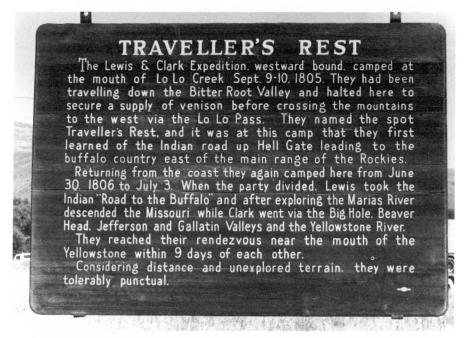

This sign along U.S. Highway 93 south of Lolo commemorates the Corps' two stays at Traveller's Rest. The actual site of the encampment was to the west and a bit north, along Lolo Creek, of where this sign is located.

they sat around the campfire telling stories and making jokes? Did they share their worries and anxieties about the coming days' journey and the snow, that everlasting snow, on those daunting mountains to the west? How late into the night did the captains and the other journal keepers write by candlelight and then pack away those precious manuscripts which they left for us to read two centuries later?

The exact location of Traveller's Rest is still under investigation. Recently, however, amateur historians and experts in locating the campsites of the Lewis and Clark Expedition are looking at a privately-owned half-acre on Mormon Creek Road in Lolo, Montana, which corresponds with the observations and descriptions of the campsite in the journals of the captains and the other journalists which they named Traveller's Rest.

Fortunately the specific area under observation has remained undisturbed by the present owners, so it is much as it was when and if the Expedition camped there on the south bank of what

The bottom land on the Deschamps' property was probably the Lolo Creek streambed at the time of the Lewis and Clark encampment. In the past 200 years, the creek has moved north to the present channel. Note the creek bank at the far left of the picture. (Photo by Jean O'Neill)

is now Lolo Creek, a mile and a half above the mouth of the creek. The creek, however, has moved its channel north since 1805-1806, but the original creek bank curves along this property.

Infrared aerial photographs, taken at the request of the Travellers' Rest Chapter of the Lewis and Clark Heritage Foundation, show tepee rings on the bench indicating that this was an Indian campsite, though not proof of the Corps of Discovery encampment.[2]

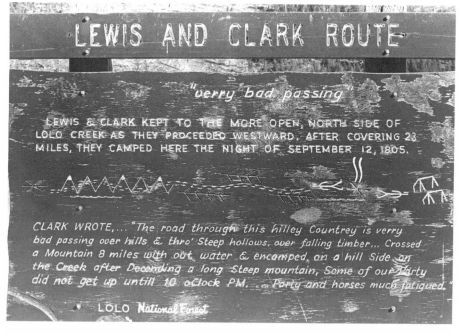

West of Traveller's Rest the Expedition mostly followed the more open hillsides along the north side of Lolo Creek, but the further it went the rougher the going became. In this area, on both sides of Lolo Pass, the mountainous going was extremely difficult, as this Lolo National Forest sign explains, and on both the outbound and return trips they labored mightily not only to overcome what Captain Clark called "verry bad passing" but also hunger and difficult, wintery weather.

CHAPTER TEN

OVER THE LOLO TRAIL WESTWARD

SEPTEMBER 11, 1805. It was a short break. Now the Corps prepared to undertake the arduous and fearful journey over the Bitterroot range along Lolo Creek and what the Nez Perce called the "buffalo trails." But two horses had disappeared and were not found until mid-afternoon. The young Nez Perce Indian who had volunteered to guide the group through the mountains grew impatient and left. How unfortunate! As the Corps would soon learn. This day the travelers advanced along the right side of Lolo Creek for about six miles and camped under some old Indian huts about a half mile east of present Woodman Creek.

Readers may ask, "Why did the Corps not go down the Clark Fork from Missoula? Joseph Whitehouse answered, *These guides tell us those waters run into the Mackenzie river as near as they can give out, but he is not acquainted that way. So we go the road he knows."[1]* The Clark Fork does, however, follow the drainage of the Columbia River basin.

Ralph Space tells us that the Nez Perce had two travel routes. The upper or "Buffalo Trail" ran along the mountain ridges and valleys; the lower trail ran to the south and was known as the "Nez Perce Trail." The Salish Indians came along this trail to fish for salmon near the present Powell Ranger station, there being no salmon in the Bitterroot or Clark Fork rivers.

Why was the passage over these trails so difficult? 1. The area is heavily timbered. 2. Snow comes early and melts late. 3. There is little game because game animals prefer to feed at the basins formed by the heads of streams. 4. The ridge follows a series of mountains and deep saddles which travelers must transverse up

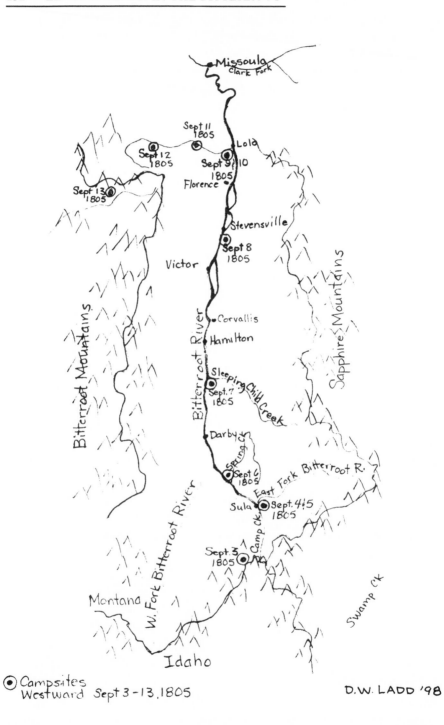

Missoula
Clark Fork

Sept 11
1805

Sept 12
1805

Lola

Sept 9, 10
1805

Florence

Sept 13
1805

Stevensville

Sept 8
1805

Victor

Bitterroot Mountains

Corvallis

Bitterroot River

Hamilton

Sapphire Mountains

Sleeping Child Creek

Sept. 7
1805

Darby

Spring Ck

Sept 6
1805

East Fork Bitterroot R.

Sula

Sept. 4, 5
1805

W. Fork Bitterroot River

Camp Ck.

Sept 3
1805

Swamp Ck

Montana

Idaho

⊙ Campsites
Westward Sept 3-13, 1805

D.W. LADD '98

and down through rough stone areas clogged with windfalls, and there was poor feed for their horses. 5. The Clearwater has fertile soil which becomes slick and muddy when wet.[2]

The morning of September 12, 1805, was frosty as the party advanced up the creek past an old Indian encampment, a sweat lodge covered with earth. Traveling grew more difficult for the men and Sacajawea, as well as being very painful for the horses. They crossed a mountain where there was no water and encamped late at night where Patrick Gass described the location as *"a very inconvenient place"*[3] about two miles east of Lolo Hot Springs. Clark wrote, *"Some of our party did not get up until 10 o'clock. Party and horses much fatigued."*[4]

September 13, 1805. The party stumbled on over steep rocky hillsides strewn with fallen timber and came upon Lolo Hot Springs, described by Clark as *"several springs issuing from large rocks of a coarse, hard grit and nearly boiling hot..near one of the springs a hole or Indian bath and roads leading in different directions.*[5] How the travelers must have longed to bathe their sore feet and muscles in these waters, but time and urgency prohibited them this luxury. Lolo Hot Springs is now and has been a popular spa and tourist attraction.

Several paths led away from the springs. Old Toby chose the wrong path and led the party three miles out of its way. The Corps continued on past many beaver dams but saw no beaver. They passed the source of Lolo Creek, crossed over the Bitterroot Divide to the Lochsa side (*Lochsa* is a Salish word meaning "rough water") from Montana into Idaho. The encampment that night was on the lower edge of what is now known as Packer Meadows. The hunters brought in one deer and four pheasants, a meager meal for thirty people.

The journey now turned into a nightmare. Hunger continued. The berries along the route were not yet ripe due to the cold. There was no game. On September 14, 1805, Captain Lewis distributed some portable soup which the men found disagreeable and decided to kill a colt and roast it. They named the last creek they had passed "Colt-killed Creek." More rough mountains continued to block the trail. No water was available; they melted snow to make the unpalatable portable soup. The horses were now weak and suffering from fatigue and lack of food. One horse fell and then another which was carrying Captain Clark's desk and small trunk. The desk broke, although, surprisingly, the horse escaped injury. The Corps struggled on through heavy timber downfalls and around knobs which constantly impeded progress.

The situation had now become desperate. On September 16, 1805, it snowed six to eight inches. The snow covered the trail and increased the misery of the travelers. Clark wrote, *"I have been wet and as cold in every part as I ever was in my life, indeed, I was at one time fearful my feet would freeze in the thin moccasins I wore....The men are cold and hungry... killed a second colt. "6* And the third and last colt on the 17th of September. The men were now dispirited, suffering from lack of food, weakness and fatigue, dysentery and skin eruptions which some historians claim could have been from venereal disease caught from the Shoshone women. The captains made a decision, probably not to their liking as they did not wish to separate. However, on September 18th Captain Clark took six men and moved on ahead of the main party under Captain Lewis. They hoped to find some game and return food to the main party. At twenty miles Clark climbed a high mountain (Sherman Peak) and looked across the ridge tops to a distant level prairie. Hope must have blazed within him, as he realized that they were now in sight of the end of their agonizing struggle through the mountains. Still that prairie was a long way off. The seven men had made thirty-two miles that day and encamped on a creek Clark named "Hungery Creek" because *"as at that place we had nothing to eat. "7*

Luckily, the next day they came across a stray horse. Not so lucky for the horse, for the men killed, dressed it and, after breakfasting, they hung the remainder for the main party to find.

The remainder of the Corps struggled on for eighteen more miles. Captain Lewis reported in his journal September 18, 1805, *"This morning we finished the last of our colt. We dined and supped on a scant portion of portable soup, a few canisters of which, a little bear oil, and about 20 pounds of candles form our stock of provisions. "8* But the next morning the party continued on, ascended a ridge of a high mountain and gazed upon the same prairie that Clark had seen the previous day. Old Toby informed them that this was the way to the Columbia River, and they could reach it on one more day's journey. Hungry and weak as they were from lack of food, this news *"greatly revived the spirits of the party."*[9]

On September 20th Captain Clark encountered the Nez Perce Indians on Weippe Prairie, in present-day Idaho, and through sign language, he made known to them that he and his men were very hungry. The Indians gave them salmon and bread made from the camas root. The men wolfed down the food and Captain Clark traded for a supply of this food which he then sent back to the main party who also stuffed themselves on the fish and camas bread.

The travails of the Corps were not over. All the men became violently ill with vomiting and dysentery, probably caused by a food poisoning or the rejection of this strange food by their bodies, which were accustomed to a straight meat diet. Captain Clark doctored them with Rush's Thunderbolts. The fact that they all survived is a credit to the strong constitutions of these rugged men, who staggered into the village of the Nez Perce Indians on Weippe Prairie more dead than alive.

When they finally regained their strength the men branded their

On the Idaho side of Lolo Pass, the Expedition viewed what seemed to be an endless chains of mountains leading them to the west and, ultimately, to the Pacific Ocean. On both the outbound and return journeys, this area was covered with snow; this portion of the Expedition's trip came close to finishing them. (Photo by Dale A. Burk)

horses and left them in the care of the Nez Perce. The Indians showed them a new way, to them, of constructing canoes by means of burning out the inside. The Corps then proceeded down the Clearwater River and, for the first time in the journey, they traveled **with** the current instead of against it. It was a dangerous voyage down the Columbia River, through rapids which nearly caused the canoes to capsize. On October 9, 1805, Captain Clark wrote: *"we were informed that our old guide and his Son had left us and had been Seen running up the river Several miles above, we Could not account the Cause of his leaveing us at this time, without receiving his pay for the Services he had rendered us, or letting us know anything of his intention. We requested the Chief to Send a horseman after our old guide to come back and receive his pay &c. Which he advised us not to do as his nation would take his things from him before he passed their camps.*[10] Nothing more is noted of Old Toby and his son in any of the surviving journals.

The Expedition continued its journey down the Columbia River to the Pacific Ocean. There they constructed quarters close to the Clatsop Indians near the mouth of the river on the south or Oregon side and hunkered down for the winter and spring 1805-1806.

By late November the Expedition had reached the mouth of the Columbia and encamped on the northern shore. However, there was little game, clothes needed replacing and the site was generally unfavorable. The Indians who visited reported a good supply of elk and timber on the southern bank, the Oregon side of the river. A vote was taken as to where to establish winter quarters. On November 24, 1805, each member of the Expedition was polled, including York and Sacajawea, whom Clark referred to as "Janey," and noted the tabulation in his journal for that day. "Janey in favour of a plac where ther is plenty of Potas." This democratic moment was the first time in American history that a woman, an Indian and a Negro slave voted.

They then journeyed back upstream to rejoin the Nez Perce Indians and claim their horses for the return journey. There this narrative will continue as the travelers journey eastward, back through the Bitterroot mountains and valley on their return trip to St. Louis and to the conclusion of the Expedition.

CHAPTER ELEVEN

THE RETURN TO THE BITTERROOT — 1806

Mdhfy ARCH 23, 1806: Spring was breaking. It was time for the Corps of Discovery to retrace its path to the home of the Nez Perce Indians who were holding their horses and who would guide them, they hoped, across those fearsome Bitterroot Mountains. Going up the Columbia against the current was hard work. Food was scarce, the Indians along the banks were starving while waiting for the salmon run. The party would gladly have eaten horsemeat, but there were only dogs to eat which nearly all the party relished, except for Captain Clark. The Indians were not only hard to deal with, they would steal anything that was unguarded which led to several nearly disastrous confrontations. At one point an Indian tried to steal Captain Lewis's dog, Seaman. The Captain went into a rage and ordered three of his men to pursue the Indians and *"fire upon them if necessary."*[1] The Indians gave up the dog, fortunately. However, Captain Lewis had risked the future of the Expedition by his angry outbursts against the pesky pilfering of the Chinook Indians.

Captain Clark went ahead, past the Dalles, and purchased four horses at the dear price of two kettles. The party continued on, finally going overland and leaving those troublesome Indians. On April 24, 1806, the travelers were in the country of the Wallawalla Indians who were relatives of the Nez Perce, and who had previously welcomed the Corps and invited them to spend a few days with them on the return trip. What a relief for the men and Sacajawea to be with friends again, and they all celebrated when Cruzatte brought out the fiddle.

On April 28, 1806, Chief Yelleppit invited the Americans to a grand feast and dance, at which he asked the guests to sing their medicine songs — meaning a powerful supernatural choral song. John Ordway reported that the men sang two songs. What were they? We are not told.

Since these men were rugged frontiersmen and army trained probably they were accustomed to popular songs, marching songs, hymns, patriotic songs. Singing and dancing were manly pastimes in those days, and we read in the journals that when Cruzatte picked up his fiddle the men danced... The first tune which comes to mind is "Yankee Doodle," which most likely was a dance tune. "Mind the music and the step,/And with the girls be handy." If not exactly a powerful medicine song, "Yankee Doodle" was well-known, lent itself to various parodies, and is traditional. Another contemporary song is a tune we recognize as "Oh, Dear, What Can the Matter Be." Cruzatte, LaBiche and Charbonneau could have joined in with "Allouette", which was probably a good marching song. Finally, a revival hymn like "Amazing Grace," written in 1748 and still popular and revered today would have been an appropriate choice.[2]

Captain Lewis wrote *"I think we can justly affirm to the honor of these people that they are the most hospitable, honest and sincere people that we have met with in our voyage.[3]*

By May 5, the travelers were back in Nez Perce country. They looked ahead and saw those mountains, those dreaded mountains, a wrenching reminder of the hardships of last September. To make matters worse, the Indians informed the captains that the winter had been harsh and much snow still clogged the mountains, valleys and ridges. The Indians also warned them that they could not make it through for at least a moon and a half. The spirits of the men went into a downward spiral. On May 8, 1806, the men who had been ordered out to hunt instead lay about camp *"without our permision of knowledge"* and the captains did *"chid them severly for their indolence and inattention".[4]* This behavior was quite unusual for the disciplined members of this expedition.

For many months the Corps had subsisted on roots, fish, horseflesh, dog meat, fowl, venison, wolf, portable soup and bear grease. Visions of roasted buffalo meat, and the foods of civilization danced in their heads and, perhaps, sugarplums did too. Tobacco lay in caches over those mountains, but now they must wait, and wait they did, but impatiently. What did the men and Sacajawea do for the next four weeks? First, they moved to an old Indian campground and set up camp at what historians call Chopunnish Camp, although the captains did not use this name (Chopunnish, or Pierced Nose, a name for the Nez Perce). Captain Lewis busied himself smoking, talking to the chiefs and repeating his message from President Jefferson that of peace and harmony among the Indian tribes, of emphasizing the power and the strength of the United States and dangling the carrot of trade in guns and goods to make the natives lives more comfortable. Note that Captain Lewis is addressing the Nez Perce not as "children" but as a sovereign nation. Little did the Nez Perce, nor Meriwether Lewis for that matter, know that once the Corps left them their lives would never be the same. Captain Lewis also expanded on his nature study and his ethnological observations of the Nez Perce.

Meanwhile, Captain Clark had become a medical practitioner who was honored among the Indians for his good medicine. Every morning patients lined up for treatment. From Clark's journal, May 12, 1806: *"I began to administer eye water and in a fiew minits had near 40 applicants with sore eyes and maney others with other complaints most common Rheumatis disorders and weakness in the back and loins particularly the womin. "*[5] (No wonder, considering the back-breaking labor expected of the Indian women, and the nonchalant attitude of the Indian culture toward child-bearing.) He treated sore eyes, ulcers, rheumatism, scrofula (tuberculosis of the lymph glands), and even paralysis and sore backs and legs. Sweat baths were a popular and effective treatment.

Sacajawea's little boy, Pomp, became *"dangerously ill, his jaw and throat is much swelled. "*[6] Clark's concern for little Pomp is evident in his journal entries from May 22 to 29, 1806, inclusive in which he reported daily on Pomp's condition and the treatment that the captain administered. Eventually Captain Clark's affection for little Pomp would prompt him to offer to rear and educate the child at his home in St. Louis when Pomp was old enough to leave his mother. Lucky Pomp. His parents agreed and left him with Captain Clark when the child was about four years old.

What were the men and Sacajawea doing during this time?

Sacajawea dug roots and probably made moccasins and repaired clothes. Was she friendly with the Nez Perce women? And did they include her in their activities? We do not know, for the journals are silent in this regard. The men, however, did mix with the natives. They raced horses, learned how the Nez Perce cared for their animals, played an Indian game called prisoner base and an American game, quoits. The exercise and stimulation served to keep them in physical condition for the rigors ahead. Meanwhile, the hunters were out trying to bag animals with only mediocre success. It was spring and time to enjoy the good weather. As they looked over their shoulders at those craggy snow-topped mountains, the men were apprehensive but anxious to proceed on. May passed into June, and the Captains and their men grew more and more impatient to move. The Nez Perce kept warning them, "There is too much snow, don't go."

However, on June 8, 1806, they bid farewell to their Nez Perce hosts with a celebration complete with dancing as Cruzatte played the fiddle. On June 10 the Corps moved on to Weippe Prairie, the camas fields where the Indians dug roots, and there the Americans made preparations to conquer the Bitterroots. Why did Captain Lewis disregard the warnings of the Indians who were very knowledgeable about these mountains? Stephen Ambrose assessed the situation: "Lewis allowed impatience to cloud his judgment. He was taking chances and violating Jefferson's orders to always be prudent so that he could carry out his number one objective, to get to the Pacific and back with the report on main features of the country."[7] But why? Because these men were explorers. Lewis still nourished the hope that maybe there was a northwest passage to the Pacific. He intended to explore the Great Falls and the Marias River.

Ambrose also observed that Lewis had been exhibiting more arrogant self-assurance than his usual display of self-confidence. The captain retained the notion of white superiority, having claimed at the Lemhi Pass in 1805 that anything squaws could do he and his men could do also. He ignored the wisdom of the Nez Perce. "He had been a mature responsible senior commander, now he was an impatient junior officer acting more on impulse than judgment."[8]

The Expedition was now well equipped with strong durable horses, thanks to the Nez Perce, and with a supply of food if not with patience and wisdom. On June 15, 1806, they began their assault on the mountains and Captain Clark wrote *"proceeded with much difficulty...road was very slipprey, and it was with great dificulty that the loaded horses could assend the hills and mountains the(y) frequently slipped down both assending and decending those steep hills. "*[9]

June 16, 1806: Clark, *"through most intolerable bad fallen timber. We found much dificulty in finding the road as it frequently covered with snow. "*[10]

June 17, 1806: Clark, *"we found it dificult and dangerous to pass the creek in consequence of its debth and rapidity, "*[11]

Decision time: 1. If they were lucky it would take them four days to reach Colt-Killed Creek before which there would be no food for the horses. 2. There was the possibility of losing horses, baggage, instruments and papers. 3. They also risked losing their way and the discoveries already made. 4. Maybe they would lose their lives.

The Corps of Discovery turned back, but not before they had carefully wrapped and cached their baggage on scaffolds. Clark wrote, *"This is the first time since we have been on this tour that we have ever been compelled to retreat or make a retragrade march. "*[12] This was a hard decision for military men.

With the decision to turn back the leaders realized the need for the Nez Perce guides. They sent Drouillard and Shannon ahead to procure guides by offering a gun, more if necessary, to procure their services. A gun was a big price. The party continued on their return trip, but after a short distance John Potts injured himself badly; a knife cut to a vein on the inner thigh. Colter's horse fell with him while crossing Hungery Creek, and the two rolled over among the rocks. Fortunately, neither was badly injured. And to complete the day, the mosquitoes were very troublesome. Ralph Space remarked that in the spring of the year the mosquitoes swarm after you. "I don't know how they endured them."[13]

The Corps then returned to Weippe Prairie to await Drouillard and Shannon and the Nez Perce guides, and to hunt which proved very good for the hunters this time.

On June 24, the Corps began its second assault on the Bitterroots, but this time with three young Nez Perce to guide them. One of the Indian guides complained of being sick, and the suspicion arose that he was trying to evade his commitment to guide. However,

Captain Lewis gave him a buffalo robe when he saw that the young lad was clad only in an elk skin and moccasins. The gift was well received, and the young man continued on with them.

June 25, 1806: The men collected the baggage that had been left on the scaffold and noted that the snow had subsided from the ten feet ten inches on the tree they had marked to about seven feet. The guides now hurried the travelers along so that they might reach good grass for the horses. They found it at Bald Mountain (Nez Perce *"kount keut"* meaning "bare hill").

June 27, 1806: On this day the young guides requested that the party stop and smoke on a hill on which the natives had erected a mound of stones about six to eight feet tall with a pine pole about fifteen feet long extending from the summit. From here the view was *"of these Stupendous mountains covered with snow like that on which we stood; we were entirely serounded by those mountains from which to one unacquainted with them it would have Seemed impossible ever to have escaped, in short without the assistance of our guides, I doubt much whether we who had present situation for the marked trees on which we had placed considerable reliance are much fewer and more difficuelt to find than we had apprehended. Those indians are most admireable pilots; we find the road wherever the snow has disappeared tho it be only for a fiew paces. ",[14]* Captain Clark.

The men and Sacajawea traveled twenty-eight miles this day. There was no meat and no grass for the horses. Dinner consisted of boiled roots and bear oil. A little better than a hungry stomach?

June 28, 1806: The horses were very hungry and tired, but by noon the guides brought the party to an abundance of grass on the side of the mountain, where they encamped. By now the travelers had discovered that they were traveling easier on the snow than without it. While slipping was inconvenient it also allowed the horses and men to slide over much of the rocks and fallen timber. The next day, June 29, 1806, the party found a deer which the hunter had left for them, a welcome change of fare from bear's oil. That day they reached Rocky Point, went down to the Lochsa River, then along the trail to the quamash flats or Packer Meadows which is a couple miles south of Lolo Pass on the divide between the Clearwater and the Bitterroot River. They reached Lolo Hot Springs that evening. This time they enjoyed the hot baths and watched the Indians jump from the hot baths into the cold creek water and back into the hot baths again.

Lolo Hot Springs was described by Captain Lewis "the principal spring is about the temperature of the warmest baths used at the hot springs in Virginia. In this bath which had been prepared by the Indians by stoping the run with stone and gravel, I bathed and remained in 19 minutes, it was with dificulty I could remain this long and it caused a prouse sweat. Two other bold springs adjacnet to this are much warmer, their heat being so great as to make the hand of a person smart extremely when immerced I think temperature of these springs about the same as the hotest of the hot springs in Virginia....I observed that the indians after remaining in the hot bath as long as they could bear it ran and plunged themselves into the creek the water of which is now as cold as ice can make it; after remaining a few minutes they returned again to the warm bath, repeating this transision several times but always ending with the warm bath." *(The temperature at Lolo Hot Springs was measured at 111 degrees Fahrenheit in 1974 and discharge measures at 180 gallons.)[15]*

The hot springs became a favorite recreation spot and a landmark for early travelers over the Lolo Trail. Later it became a resort and vacationing spot particularly lauded for its health giving waters. Lolo Hot Springs resort is privately owned and continues to be a popular spot easily accessible from Montana Highway 12. However, there never was a Fort Lolo or a Fort Lolo Hot Springs.

There was still a difficult and dangerous trail ahead where Captain Lewis' horse slipped. Lewis was knocked off and fell forty feet before he could stop his descent by grabbing a branch. *"The horse was near falling on me but fortunately recovers and we both escape unhurt,"[16]* Captain Lewis wrote on June 30, 1806. That evening the Corps arrived at Traveller's Rest. Whereas they had been eleven days on the trail going west the previous September, these young Nez Perce men had guided them 156 miles in just five days, led the horses to grass every day but one, had exhibited a fine sense of direction and found the trail even under ten feet of snow. When Lewis wrote that not even Drouillard could find his way in these mountains, he was giving his Nez Perce guides an extraordinary compliment.

CHAPTER TWELVE

TRAVELLER'S REST — 1806

T RAVELLER'S REST LIVED up to its name in 1806, a place of rest, three days of rest and relaxation for the men of the Corps of Discovery who breathed sighs of relief and satisfaction. They had completed the trek to the Pacific Ocean and back again across the Bitterroots with less inconvenience, hardship and hunger than they had experienced on the westward journey in 1805, thanks to their Nez Perce guides. Captain Clark remarked that in leaving *"those tremendous mountanes behind us — in passing of which we have experiensed Cold and hunger of which I shall ever remember.*[1] The waters were high in the Bitterroot Valley in June and early July in 1806. The men realized that fording the swollen waterways would be dangerous, and that there would be trying days unpacking and drying out baggage.

Captain Clark noted in 1806, that on July 3rd the snow persisted 1/5 down the Bitterroot Mountains....Many geologists subscribe to a "Little Ice Age" which was on the decline at the time of the Corps visit, and entirely over circa 1850. One cited bit of supporting evidence: what is now Glacier National Park had circa 1850 about 150 glaciers...now there are 17 (ballpark numbers).[2]

But for the moment, the Indians raced their horses and the men amused themselves by having footraces with the young Indian guides who proved to be strong and athletic. Shields was kept busy enough repairing and caring for the guns, of which one had been "birst" near the muzzle. This was then exchanged with the Indian to whom they had given a gun a few days earlier. Captain Lewis wrote an extensive description of the prairie dog which he referred to as "*barking squirrel*". Fortunately, the hunters succeeded in bringing in twelve deer on July 1, and two more on July 2. Both Captain Clark and Patrick Gass complained of the mosquitoes.

Traveller's Rest Today

The exact location of Traveller's Rest has recently been pinpointed by experts in locating the campsites of the Lewis and Clark Expedition. One of these experts, Dr. Robert T. Bergantino, hydrogeologist at the Montana Bureau of Mines and Technology, at Butte, Montana, has spent the last twenty-five years constructing maps and locating the campsites of the Corps of Discovery on the journey west to the Pacific Coast and on the return. Dr. Bergantino reminds us that the Corps left no markers so the location of the various campsites is not absolute, but as close as can be ascertained from the descriptions in the journal — and after nearly two hundred years have passed .

According to the journals, the coordinates of latitude and longitude recorded by the Expedition and also by Clark's map indicate that the site of Traveller's Rest was on the south bank of Lolo Creek about a mile and a half upstream from where the creek empties into the Bitterroot River. This location matches the property owned by Ernie and Pat Deschamps. Recent infrared aerial photographs taken for the Traveller's Rest Chapter of the Lewis and Clark Trail Heritage Foundation, show tepee rings on the bench to the south, which are proof of an historic Indian campsite there, though not necessarily proof of the Expeditions two stops at the site. Lolo Creek has diverted to the north of where it probably was in 1805-1806, but the creek bed and banks are still visible.

Fortunately, the Deschamps have not disturbed the land and have used it only for horse pasture. The creek bed and banks are there to see. Traveller's Rest is largely undisturbed and easily accessible at Lolo, Montana, in the Bitterroot Valley.

Here at Traveller's Rest on July 1, Captain Lewis collected and preserved several plant specimens, of which four had not been yet described. One was the perennial plant native to Montana, the "bitterroot," which was named *Lewisa rediviva* in his honor. It is the most celebrated of all the plants brought back by Lewis — as previously pointed out, it is the state flower of Montana, and its name has been given to the Bitterroot Valley and the major mountain range to its west.

Whitetail deer.

The Nez Perce guides were anxious to return to their home, but they were persuaded to travel with Captain Lewis and his party and show them the right route along the trail to the great falls of the Missouri. The captains gave a small medal to the son of the chief of the Nez Perce, who had been kind to the Americans. Captain Lewis received the name "Yo-me-kol-lick" which means "white bear skin foalded (folded)." It was a tribute to be named after a grizzly bear.[3] The other Indians received red ribbons and one Indian presented a horse to Captain Lewis with the request that he show the horse to the Pahkees as a sign that they wished to be at peace.

On July 2, 1806, the captains put into effect the plan they had devised over the last winter. At Traveller's Rest, the party would split. Captain Lewis would take nine men — Gass, Drouillard, Joseph and Reubin Field, Werner, Frazer, Thompson, McNeal and Goodrich — and seventeen horses and travel north on the trail of the Nez Perce to the great falls of the Missouri. Captain Clark would guide the remaining members of the party and the horses, and proceed south through the Bitterroot Valley, over the Continental Divide to their cache on the upper Beaverhead River, and thence to the Three Forks of the Missouri.

Captain Lewis was to split his command again, upon arrival at the Missouri River taking his most competent men on an exploration of the Marias River and leaving the others to prepare for the portage around the great falls. Meanwhile, Sergeant Ordway, who traveled with Captain Clark to the Three Forks of the Missouri, would command a detachment of ten men in the canoes which were recovered from the cache there, and proceed down the Missouri to assist with the portage. Portage completed, they would then pick up Captain Lewis and his group at the mouth of the Marias and all would descend to the confluence of the Missouri and the Yellowstone, where they would reunite with Captain Clark.

Meanwhile Captain Clark and his group would travel from the Three Forks to the Yellowstone River, where their plan was to build canoes. He would detach Sergeant Pryor and two men to take the horses overland to the Mandan Village where the horses could be used for trade. Also, Sergeant Pryor was to deliver an important letter to Hugh Heney, a Canadian trader whom the captains hoped to enlist as an intermediary with the Sioux. Captain Clark would then lead his group, including Sacajawea and her baby, down the river in the canoes to the junction of the Yellowstone and the Missouri, there to join Captain Lewis and his men in five to six weeks. It was an ambitious and risky plan, depending on close timing, and the ability of the men to act quickly, responsibly and ingeniously. This was dangerous country, the land of the Blackfeet, Crows, and the grizzly bear. Could these small squads, split from the main party, carry out this plan? The stories of their adventures are written in their journals.

CHAPTER THIRTEEN

RETRACING THE BITTERROOT VALLEY — JULY 1806

DECISION MADE, ARRANGEMENTS completed. The captains had decided to separate and divide the Corps to complete their explorations. Captain Lewis chose nine men to accompany him on an exploration north over the Continental Divide to the Missouri River, which the Indians had described to them and had also claimed could be made in four or five days. This journey would take them deep into Blackfeet territory. Their Indian friends warned them of the hostile and aggressive behavior of the fierce and feared Blackfeet. Nevertheless, Lewis was confident in himself and in his men and eager to explore the Marias River in northwest Montana. He still nourished the hope that there he might find the long-sought passage to the Pacific. Captain Clark would take the remainder of the party up the Bitterroot River Valley, over the Continental Divide eastward to the valley of the Yellowstone River, about a five hundred mile journey. The captains expected to meet, on the Missouri, in about five to six weeks. Their plans were both dangerous and ambitious.

Captain Lewis, July 3, 1806, wrote, *"I took leave of my worthy friend and companion, Captain Clark and the party that accompanyed him. I could not avoid feeling much concern on this occasion although I hoped this seperation was only momentary."*[1] What emotions did the men and Sacajawea feel as they parted? The experiences they had shared had bonded them into a unit as close and intimate as a family. Did they wonder if they would see their friends again? Had Captain Lewis known, he would have had as much concern for himself and for his own party.

Captain Lewis, his party of nine men, five Nez Perce guides and seventeen horses forded Traveller's Rest Creek (Lolo) about a half-

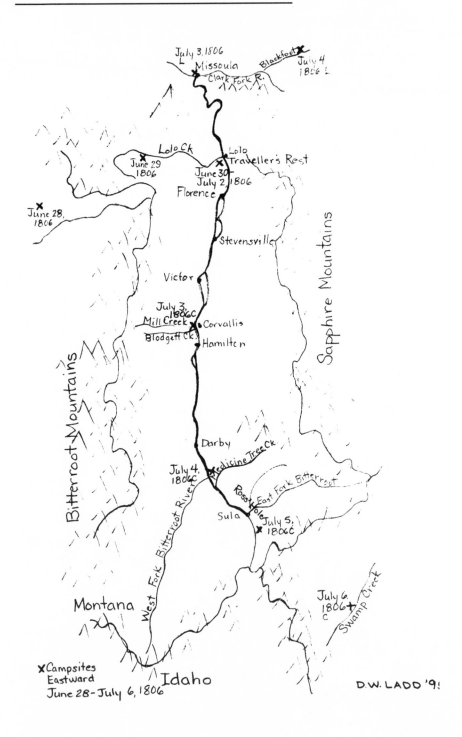

July 3, 1806
L
Missoula
Blackfoot
July 4
1806 L
Clark Fork R.

Lolo Ck
June 29
1806
Lolo
Traveller's Rest
June 30
July 2, 1806
Florence

June 28,
1806

Stevensville

Sapphire Mountains

Victor

July 3,
1806C
Mill Creek
Corvallis
Blodgett Ck.
Hamilton

Bitterroot Mountains

Darby

Medicine Tree Ck.
July 4,
1806C
West Fork Bitterroot River
Ross Hole
East Fork Bitterroot
Sula
July 5,
1806C

July 6.
1806
C
Swamp Creek

Montana

Idaho

XCampsites
Eastward
June 28–July 6, 1806

D.W. LADD '91

mile below their encampment and proceeded down the west side of the Bitterroot River to its junction with the Clark Fork. They then continued downstream along the river, which was about 150 yards wide, for about two more miles before the Indian guides recommended a good place for crossing. The Indians tugged their baggage along in little deerskin basins as they swam their horses across the river, followed by the remaining horses. Captain Lewis and his men gathered up the scarce timber in the area and constructed three small rafts. After three hours and three trips across, the rafts had moved a mile and a half down the river. Captain Lewis and two remaining men started across at a very difficult and dangerous crossing where the river was swollen, rapid, crowded with small islands and submerged willows. Captain Lewis was swept from the raft into the dangerous, powerful current. The raft sank, but the two men did reach shore, and Captain Lewis managed to save himself and to swim to safety. The travelers continued eastward to the confluence of Grant Creek with the Clark Fork River and encamped about three miles west of the present city of Missoula. Lewis wrote that the mosquitoes at the spot were so bad, literally torturing the horses so much that the men built fires and placed the animals in the smoke. The following day, the fourth of July, the Nez Perce guides said farewell after directing Captain Lewis toward the *"river of the road to the buffaloe, the Cokalahishkit,* (the Big Blackfoot) and the road to the great falls of the Missouri, which they claimed even a white man could find. However, the Indians feared for their friends, that they would be "cut down" by the Pahkees (the Blackfeet), their bitter enemy.

Three weeks later, on July 26, 1806, he, Drouillard and the Field brothers were exploring the Marias River in the Two Medicine country. Here they met eight young Blackfeet. That night the Indians and the Americans shared camp and smoked while Captain Lewis gave his peace talk. He told them that he had organized their traditional enemies, the Shoshone, the Nez Perce and others into an American alliance and intended to offer them rifles. Next, he invited them to join the American empire, which, he assured them, would give them a better deal than they now had with the British who were supplying them with weapons. The next morning the Blackfeet attempted to steal rifles and drive off the horses. A confrontation occurred in which two of the young Indians were killed. Realizing their danger if a band of Blackfeet arrived to pursue them, the Americans hastily retreated, traveling 100 miles in less than twenty-four hours. However, when Lewis's message reached the Blackfeet, that tribe realized that their superiority over their unarmed tribal victims on the prairies and in the valleys was being challenged. This, along with the killing of the two young Indians, aroused the enmity of the Blackfeet, clouding their relations with and increasing their hostility toward Americans.

Meanwhile, Captain Clark with the remaining members of the Corps, twenty-two men, Sacajawea and her child, and fifty horses turned south along the west side of the Bitterroot River, which was now so high with snow-melt, that crossing it was impossible. The valley bloomed with lush spring growth and with a sweet clover that the horses relished. However, the creeks too were swollen with spring melt-off and provided a challenge to these experienced horsemen to ford them. Not only had this party struggled through snowdrifts ten to twelve feet deep only a few weeks before, but now those melting snows threatened their life and limb. Clark wrote that *"we crossed large Creeks which comes roleing their Currents with Velocity into the river."[2]* Moulton notes that they had crossed Mormon, Carlton, One Horse, Sweeney and Bass creeks before they "nooned" it, probably on the north bank of Kootenai Creek about where Highway 93 crosses the creek, according to Dr. Robert Bergantino. On their way they had passed the point at which the Corps had crossed the river from the east to the west bank on their way to Traveller's Rest on September 9, 1805.

Between Carlton and One Horse Creeks there is a small town today, Florence, Montana, which was first called "One Horse" and then re-named "Florence" in 1880 for Mrs. Florence Hammond, the wife of A.B. Hammond. Mr. Hammond, owner and founder of the Missoula Mercantile Company in Missoula, purchased lumber in this areas and then built sawmills to process it.

After grazing their horses the travelers resumed their journey up the valley where Clark reported seeing great numbers of deer, a bear, the burrowing squirrel and very troublesome *"musquetors"*. However, they also experienced the warmth and beauty of early summer, and observed cottonwood, birch and sweet willow trees, plants and grasses. But the scenic beauty of the rugged Bitterroots to the west seemed to be lost on these travelers.

Now the melting snows rushed down the canyons, threatening to engulf and carry them along swift currents and into dangerous situations. Captain Clark wrote *"those Creeks take their rise in the mountains to the West which mountains is at this time Covered with snow for about 1/5 of the way from their tops downwards. Some Snow is also to be Seen on the high points and hollows of the Mountains to the east of us."[3]* (Sapphire Mountains)

Today's residents of and travelers through the Bitterroot Valley wonder at the majesty and rugged beauty of these same mountains. These peaks may be clothed in white and indigo on a cold winter day, change to variegated greens against blue skies in summer, then shimmer in the red and gold tones of fall. They can wear a shroud

The Lewis and Clark Expedition fascinated the late artist Sandy Ingersoll of Stevensville, Montana, who did this major work of the Expedition "Dining in the Bitterroot" at one of their stops just outside where the town of Stevensville is now located. (Photo by Dale Burk)

of fog in the morning and emerge in shining splendor in the afternoon as sunlight plays with lights and shadows along the ridges and valleys. Majestic peaks, such as St. Mary and Trapper, are hosts to hikers in summer, sturdy serious hikers. For although trails exist in criss-cross patterns along their heights, these mountains are essentially much the same as when the members of the Expedition first saw them. There are few places in America along the Lewis and Clark trail that are not plowed, built upon, covered with concrete or permanently changed, but in Montana one may still look off into the distance and see the same views that the Corps of Discovery described when they too traveled through this valley and over these mountains.

From Kootenai Creek, the travelers continued their trek through the valley across Big Creek, Sweathouse, Bear and Fred Burr Creeks. They camped that night on Blodgett Creek near present-day city of Hamilton.

Between Sweathouse Creek and the North Fork of Bear Creek a little town grew up. It was first called "Sweathouse" because of the number of Indian sweat lodges in the area around the creek.

Then it was renamed "Garfield" for President James Garfield, who was assassinated in 1881, and finally "Victor" in honor of the Salish Chief Victor, son of Chief Three Eagles, the same Chief Three Eagles who first spotted members of the Corps of Discovery as they approached the Salish Indian encampment at Ross' Hole, September 4, 1805.

July 4, 1806. The swift-rushing creeks, swollen with melt and floating debris, continued to challenge the travelers as they searched for places to ford them. Captain Clark: *"the last Creek or river which we pass'd was So deep and the water So rapid that Several of the horses were Sweped down Some distance and the Water run over Several articles...the water was So Strong, alto'the debth was not much above the horses belly, emensely rapid has great decnt."*[4] This was probably Lost Horse Creek, which is still a formidable creek. Many of the natural wild and rushing creeks that the Expedition crossed are now quite tamed by dams and irrigation ditches which divert and channel their waters to various agricultural farms, orchards and ranches in the valley.

This was Independence Day, and these men were not too far removed from the Revolutionary War. *"A day Commonly Scelebrated by my Country" Captain Clark wrote.*[5] At noon the party stopped and enjoyed a saddle of venison and Mush of Cows (cous roots) then proceeded on their journey. Two years before, in 1804, they had celebrated this day on the Missouri River near Kansas City by discharging a swivel gun at sunrise and in the evening. Swivel guns were mounted on their keel boat and one on each of the pirogues. The men were given an extra issue of whiskey on that day and probably accompanied the draughts with toasts and song. The following year, 1805, the Corps was engaged in the portage around the great falls in Montana, but Patrick Gass described their Fourth of July celebration as *"A fine day...about 4 o'clock in the afternoon, when we drank the last of our spirits in celebrating the day, and amused ourselves with dancing till 9 o'clock at night."*[6] And they killed seven buffalo and saw twenty-five wolves in one pack.

When the party left Blodgett Creek they passed along the western outskirts of what is now the town of Hamilton. The copper baron, Marcus Daly, had this town planned and plotted to his specification by James Hamilton, for whom the town is named. Daly acquired vast lumber tracts in the region to support his mines in Butte. As has been noted, Daly also built an estate and mansion, Riverside, a stock farm and racing stables for his horses. This is the home of the Rocky Mountain Laboratory, which was established to research Rocky Mountain Spotted Fever in 1873, and is now a laboratory for infectious diseases. Hamilton is a trade center for the Bitterroot Valley and the county seat of Ravalli County.

The travelers proceeded on up the west side of the Bitterroot River over more rapid creeks, probably Rock, Tin Cup and Chaffin Creeks, and camped on the north side of the West Fork near its junction with the Bitterroot. Hunters killed four deer. That day they traveled thirty miles.

July 5, 1806. Colter pointed out a ford across the West Fork at which there were five channels separated by small islands. The party passed over these without danger, but water seeped into Captain Clark's trunk and portmanteau, wetting the sea otter skins and other articles including medicines and roots. Soon they struck the East

Fork and noted that it was not much higher than the previous fall. Further up the creek they found the road they had passed down going west and crossed over to the east side of the East Fork. Shannon killed a deer, but left his tomahawk there and was quickly dispatched by his captain to go back and retrieve it. After drying their articles the party crossed a mountain and valley into Ross' Hole near present Sula, where the Corps had met the Salish on the previous year. Two miles up the creek they camped on Camp Creek near the present Sula Ranger Station and U.S. Highway 93 which was some two miles southeast of the camp of September 4-5, 1805. Shields was sent out to examine the road and he reported back that the best way appeared to be a plain beaten path which was the route the Salish had taken on their way to hunt buffalo.

Captain Clark decided, *"as this rout of the Oat lash shoots can be followed it will evidently Shorten our rout at least 2 days and as the indians informed me last fall a much better rout than the one we came out. At all events I am deturmined to make the attempt and follow their trail if possible if I can prosue it my rout will be nearer and much better than the one we Came from the Shoshones & if I should not be able to follow their road; our rout can't possibly be much wors.*[7]

July 6, 1806, Clark's journal: *"Some frost this morning the last night was so cold that I could not Sleep....proceeded up the Creek (Camp) and left the road which we came on last fall to our right and assended a ridge with a gentle Slope to the dividing mountain which Seperates the waters...prosueing the rout of the Oat lash shute band which we met last fall."*[8]

The Corps had now passed over the Continental Divide, into the headwaters of the great Missouri River drainage, at Gibbon Pass which was the route taken by the Salish when they crossed to the Big Hole region. The travelers continued on down Glade Creek (Trail Creek) where they observed quawmash (camas) just beginning to bloom, and the appearance of old buffalo roads and some buffalo heads. (Nicolas Biddle made mention of this as "proving that formerly Buffs (mountain bison) roved there & also that this is the best route, for the Buffs and the Indians always have the best route & here both were joined.")[9]

> *In 1877 a band of Nez Perce Indians under Chief Joseph had just passed through the Bitterroot Valley on their way to safety and a new home. They were attacked in a bloody battle at the Big Hole Battlefield on August 7, 1877, in an assault led by Col. John Gibbon, for whom Gibbon Pass is named.*
>
> *Elliot Coues makes the argument that this pass should be named "Clark's Pass," which Captain Lewis never made. Also, Captain Clark never crossed the Lewis and Clark Pass from the Big Blackfoot to the Dearborn River, but both captains did pass the Divide over what is now called Lemhi Pass.[10] Interesting, but the present names will probably remain as Coues observation was made over a hundred years ago in 1893.[11]*

Captain Clark's party had now left the Bitterroot Valley, its river and the mountain ranges encircling it.

Historian K. Ross Toole noted that the Expedition had traveled farther into Montana and spent more time there than any other area, and that it had made its most important discoveries and had its greatest crisis there. "Although they left only the ashes of their campfires behind Montana (and the Bitterroot Valley) would never be the same again,"[12] Toole observed.

Historic point — the Marias River (left) flows into the Missouri River in northcentral Montana. It was at this point, in July of 1806, that Captain Meriwether Lewis and his men, after their encounter with the Blackfeet on the upper Marias, at Cut Bank Creek, and a wild all-night, 100-mile ride in rough country, arrived at precisely the same time as the Corps of Discovery party coming downriver by piroque got there. This thereby enabled a hasty, and safe, exit from this country, and escape from the vengeful Blackfeet they believed were pursuing them. On the upriver journey in 1805, it was here that Lewis and Captain Clark had made the crucial decision that the Marias, at that time swollen with runoff water and almost equal in size to the other channel, was not the main fork and the Expedition instead had properly gone "south" up the fork that was soon proven to be the main river when they reached the great falls of the Missouri. This point was then called, and is now known as, "Decision Point." An easily-accessible overview provides an excellent view of the scene. (Photo by Dale A. Burk)

CHAPTER FOURTEEN

CAPT. CLARK'S JOURNEY FROM THE BITTERROOT TO THE YELLOWSTONE

CAPTAIN CLARK AND the members of his party shook the dust of the Bitterroots from their moccasins and proceeded on through the Big Hole Basin. Did they sigh with relief to be through with those *"emence mountains"* where they had experienced hunger and severe hardship? Did Sacajawea look back knowing she would never return to her people? Did exhilaration sweep through the group now that they had survived and were on the way home?

However, they had left open the door to the wilderness that was the Bitterroot and defined a path into the land of the *"red willow."* Before they would reach St. Louis, fur traders and adventurers would be on their way up the Missouri to find the paths in search of the wealth the beaver would bring them. Although the mission of the Lewis and Clark Expedition was to bring peace between the Indian tribes and to coerce them into the orbit of the United States of America so that commerce could flourish, peace did not come. Trade, however, did. By the end of the century the fur traders, with the assistance of the Indians themselves, would have claimed the beaver and introduced whiskey and disease to the natives. In order to obtain the "medicine" they had heard that the blackrobes possessed, the Salish invited the Jesuit missionaries to establish a mission among them. They became Christians at the expense of their culture. The priests attempted to change their new converts from nomad hunters to farmers in an effort to prepare them for the onslaught that was coming. Finally, the settlers and land grabbers came and with the aid of the "benevolent" white father and the government in Washington, and through fraudulent and unkept treaties, they pushed the trusting and generous Salish people from their ancestral home in the Bitterroot Valley onto the present Flathead reservation north of Missoula.

Chief Charlo, son of Victor lamented: "We were happy when he (the white man) first came. We first thought he came from the light; but he comes like the dusk of evening now, not like the dawn of morning. He comes like a day that has passed, and night enters our future with him."[1]

Traveling was easier now and game more plentiful. The travelers continued through the Big Hole Valley where a century later huge cattle ranches would dominate the land. At Jackson, near Wisdom, Montana, Sergeant Pryor and John Shields tested the heat of the hot spring and cooked their strips of meat in twenty-five to thirty minutes. They were now in Beaverhead County, Montana, and soon in the Beaverhead Valley, known to the Indians as the *Hane-pompy-hah*. Captain Clark noted, *"great numbers of Beaver lying on the Shores in the Sun."*[2] Not for long could those beaver relax. Soon trappers, encouraged by the reports brought back by the members of this party, would converge upon the *"emence"* number of beavers which would be nearly swallowed by the demand and greed of the fur trade.

Manuel Lisa built the first fur post in Montana, 1807. By 1834 the demand for beaver declined as new textiles came on the market. The streams were depleted, and the trappers moved on to become guides and scouts. The white hunters found buffalo hides easier to come by and more profitable.[3]

July 8, 1806, the travelers arrived at Camp Fortunate where, the summer before, they had sunk their canoes and cached their specimens and supply of tobacco. Captain Clark wrote, *"most of the Party with me being Chewers of Tobacco became So impatient to be chewing it that they Scarcely gave themselves time to take their Saddles off their horses before they were off to the deposit."*[4]

Camp Fortunate, where the full party had first stopped on August 17, 1805, was on the east bank of the Beaverhead River below the forks in Beaverhead County, Montana. The site is now under Clark Canyon Reservoir just above the dam.[5] *They passed*

*Grasshopper Creek near Bannack, Montana, where in 1862 gold
was discovered. In the first year over five million dollars was taken
from the gulch and the town of Bannack was later the first capitol
of the Territory of Montana.*[6]

The men now raised the canoes, dried them out and on July
10, 1806, a day the water froze, the travelers continued now by
canoe and horseback down the Beaverhead (called the Jefferson in the
Journals) to where this river joins the Jefferson and flows on to the
Three Forks. The journals have descriptions of more beaver noisily
flapping their tails, of streams choked with beaver ponds, large herds
of elk, antelope, rattlesnake, bear, otter — in short, a country rich
with wildlife and also inhabited by hordes of troublesome
"mosquitors." They passed Beaverhead rock, a landmark for
Sacajawea, who was now familiar with this country and gave advice
and direction to Captain Clark. *"The indian woman who has been of
great service to me as a pilot through this country recommends a gap
in the mountain more South which I will cross,"*[7] he wrote in his
journal.

The party reached the Three Forks and on July 13, 1806, met
Sergeant Ordway with the horses. The party now split. Captain Clark
dispatched Sergeant Ordway with Collins, Colter, Cruzatte, Howard,
Lepage, Potts, Weiser, Whitehouse and Willard in six canoes down
the Missouri river to meet Captain Lewis at the great falls.

Captain Clark, Sergeant Pryor, Shields, Gibson,
Charbonneau, Sacajawea, their child, York and forty-nine horses and
a colt continued on horseback in a southeasterly direction following
the directions of Sacajawea. They crossed and recrossed the Gallatin
River in Gallatin County, Montana, and near the present vicinity of
Bozeman, crossed over the *"gap in the mountains"* indicated by
Sacajawea, and into Park County. They reached their goal, the
Rochejhone River (Yellowstone) near present-day Livingston,
Montana, at 2:00 p.m. on July 15, 1806, having traveled forty-eight
miles from the Three Forks according to Captain Clark's
calculations.

*Scholars of the Journals of the Lewis and Clark Expedition
have commented on the accuracy of the measurements and distances
recorded by Captain Clark. Elliot Coues commented on Clark's*

"Course Distance and Remarks from the Three Forks of the Missouri to the River Rochejhone where it enters the Rocky Mountains." Coues commented that *"His distances are very near those since determined by accurate survey."*[8]

An interesting note occurs in Clark's journal, on July 16, 1806: *"two of the horses was So lame owing to their feet being worn quit Smooth and to the quick, the hind feet was much worst I had Mockersons made of green Buffalow Skin and put on their feet which Seams to relieve them very much in passing over the Stoney plains.*[9]

On July 18, Gibson was thrown from his horse, fell on a snag and was severely injured. He could not continue on horseback. The party halted, constructed two canoes, which they lashed together. Unfortunately, on July 21 they found that half their horses had been stolen. This was a big loss as by now the only commodity they had for trading was the horses. Captain Clark instructed Sergeant Pryor, accompanied by Shannon, Hall and Windsor, to take the remaining horses overland to the Mandan villages. There he was to contact Hugh Heney, a trader to the Sioux Indians, and deliver a letter requesting him to act as an intermediary with the Sioux and to use the horses for trade if necessary. However, the letter was never delivered for on the second night out the horses were stolen, probably by the very accomplished horse thieves, the Crow Indians. What now? They were stranded and on foot in the wilderness. With the ingenuity they had acquired throughout their travels, the three men killed buffalo, used the skins to construct Mandan style "bull boats" and proceeded down the Yellowstone where they caught up with Captain Clark and his party on August 8, 1806.

About twenty-eight miles northeast of today's Billings, Montana, a large sandstone outcropping bears an inscription "Wm. Clark, July 25, 1806." Captain Clark wrote in his journal, "200 feet high and 400 paces in secumpherance and only accesaable on one side...The natives have ingraved on the face of this rock the figures of animals etc. near which I marked my name and the deay of the month and year."

This is Pompey's Pillar, which was originally named Pompey's Tower by Captain Clark for Sacajawea's small son, Jean Baptiste Charbonneau, whom Captain Clark affectionately called "Pomp." This is the only known extant physical evidence remaining of the historic journey of the Corps of Discovery. The site is now a state park under government management. The signature is preserved and protected under a glass screen.

From there on the trip down the river was uneventful. The travelers arrived at the mouth of the river on August 3, 1806, but the mosquitoes were intolerable, and they moved down the river. On August 11 they encountered two trappers, Joseph Dickson and Forrest Hancock, the first white men they had seen since April 1805. The news the trappers gave them was that the Missouri River Indians were fighting again. The peace had not held. On August 12 Captain Lewis and his men caught up with and joined Captain Clark and his party. The Corps of Discovery was again reunited.

CHAPTER FIFTEEN

THE LAST LEG — AUGUST-SEPTEMBER, 1806

T HE WIND WAS at their back, as the men of the Corps of Discovery dipped their paddles exuberantly into the waters of the Missouri, which hastened their canoes downriver with the current toward St. Louis and home. They were all together again and jubilant, as they, with Sacajawea and Pomp, embarked upon the last leg of their historic journey. They could rejoice now; they had reached the Pacific Ocean, had discovered that there was no northwest passage to that western shore and thus, to the Orient, and had put an end to the dream of men for more than 300 years.

However, they were returning with answers to most of the questions President Jefferson had asked. They had blazed the trail, had proven themselves and had all lived to return home with tales of adventures and of a wilderness that was beyond the dreams and expectations of any one of them.

On August 14, 1806, the travelers were once again at the Mandan villages in North Dakota, among their Indian friends with whom they had wintered in 1804. Because Captain Lewis was still recovering from his wound and was unable to walk, Captain Clark took over the diplomatic endeavors to persuade the Indian chiefs to return to Washington with them and to meet the great Father, the President. Captain Clark repeated the message of peace among the tribes and promised them protection from their enemies by the new owners of the land, the government of the United States of America. In exchange the Indian chiefs were assured that they would receive many presents and goods from this beneficent government in exchange for trade in furs and pelts.

It was a hard sell. The Indians feared being killed by their enemies, the Sioux, but finally, the Mandan Chief Sheheke, agreed to go — but only with the provision that his family accompany him.

Here at the Mandan villages, Charbonneau, Sacajawea and little Jean Baptiste left their friends with whom they had lived and shared so many adventures over the last year and a half. The little family remained behind but with the promise that they would bring "little Pomp," now nineteen months old, to St. Louis when he was old enough to be reared and educated by Captain Clark.

John Colter asked that he be discharged so that he could return to the Montana beaver streams with the fur traders, Dickson and Hancock. His discharge was approved, provided that no other member of the party make a similar request. They all agreed and Colter left with good wishes from his friends for success and "bon" adventure.

Colter departed but would soon walk into the pages of history as the first man to describe the natural wonders of the area now encompassed by Yellowstone National Park, nicknamed "Colter's Hell" and of the beauty of the Tetons and Jackson Hole, Wyoming. John Colter's name would also be permanently inscribed in western folklore as the mountain man who, when captured by the Blackfeet, saved his own life by winning a foot race against the fleetest of their Indian braves. Then, naked, barefoot and half dead, Colter scrambled for 200 miles to help and safety, always fearful that the dreaded Blackfeet were pursuing him.

On August 17, 1806, the travelers continued their journey down the Missouri, stopped to visit the Arikaras at their village in South Dakota, smoked the pipe, and ate corn, beans and squash. Captain Clark heard their complaints, attempted to ease relations between them and their neighbors, tried again to assure them of the greatness and protective attitude of the United States government and invited the chiefs to return with them to visit the great Father in Washington. However, the Arikaras were anxiously awaiting the return of their chief who had already gone to visit the great Father. Unfortunately, they would learn eventually that their chief had died. Captain Clark had heard of the chief's death from some traders traveling upstream, but wisely chose not to disclose the news to the Arikaras.

As the travelers continued their journey downriver, they passed the feared South Dakotan Teton Sioux, the Lakota, who invited them to stop, but the Captains rebuffed these Sioux because of the troubles they had encountered with them the previous year on their way upstream. The weather was unsettled, rain, cold, windy and totally disagreeable. Nearly every entry in the journals those days complained of the "*musquitors,*" the pesky enemy of the Expedition for most of their journey.

On September 1, 1806, they met and had a friendly council with the Yankton Sioux and on September 4, they visited the grave of Sergeant Charles Floyd, who had died en route, on August 4, 1804, and was buried near Sioux City, Iowa. More traders met the returning adventurers and cheered them with whiskey. What grins and warmth that must have engendered! The men were also able to exchange their leather for linen shirts and beaver for *Corse* hats. How anxious they must have been as they met more and more traders who gave them news of the nation, plied them with whiskey, sugar, chocolate and other delectables in return for all the information about the beaver the lynx, the otter, grizzly bear, buffalo, the Indians, the rivers and the country. Within months the passage to the west which was now laid open by the Lewis and Clark Expedition would become the route of the traders, the entrepreneurs and then the settlers who surged westward spilling over the Indian territories on their way to wealth and development. President Jefferson still had hopes of the return of the Expedition, they learned, but most of the country thought them dead or slaves in the mines of the Spanish.

Because Spain still had claims on the Pacific Northwest, the Spanish attempted to stop the Expedition. At that time it was generally believed that the headwaters of the Missouri were much closer to New Mexico than is actually the case. Between 1804 and 1806 the government of New Spain sent at least four expeditions onto the Great Plains to intercept the Lewis and Clark Expedition. The first and last came within several days travel of the Americans but were defeated by logistical problems or by lack of cooperation from the Indians.[1]

Captain Lewis had now recovered and had the pleasure of collecting plant specimen again. On September 17, 1806, he met an old acquaintance, Captain John McClallen, who was surprised to see them and rejoiced by giving them more whiskey and delectables.

Although it is not verifiable, there has been speculation that Captain McClallen established a trading post in Salish territory and quite possibly was killed there by the Blackfeet, along with Pierre Cruzatte, Joseph Fields, and John Thompson, in 1810.

Another trading party feted the travelers with more enticements. Songs were sung, stories told and maybe Cruzatte accompanied the dancers. Who knows — but the homecoming celebration had begun!

Toward the end of the journey some of the men developed sore eyes, possibly from sunburn or from an infection, and were unable to take part at rowing, but with growing enthusiasm they speeded on toward St. Louis, subsisting only on pawpaws but happily going home. On September 20, 1806, they saw cows and shouted for joy. At St. Charles, they observed ladies and gentlemen strolling on the river bank and saluted the town with several volleys from their firearms. Along the way, townspeople greeted them with cheers and hospitality, and on the twenty-third of September the travelers arrived at St. Louis at *"12 oClock amidst cheers from the crowdes gathered on the riverbank."* The Corps of Discovery had returned after being gone two years and five months and having covered over seven thousand miles. On September 26, 1806, Captain Clark wrote his final journal entry, *"a fine morning we commenced wrighting &c."*[2]

APPENDIX

GLOSSARY OF TERMS

Brarow — Badger

Choppunish — The name Lewis & Clark used for the Nez Perce.

Cokahlar colsh: (Nez Perce) — "Buffalo river falls"

Cokahlar ishkit River: (Nez Perce) — "River of the road to the buffalo" Indian name for Blackfoot River

Culturally Scarred (Modified) Trees — Trees (generally pines) that were peeled by the Indians for their use of the cambium layer, leaving a particularly shaped scar.

Camp Fortunate (where canoes were left) — Forks of Beaverhead River, Beaverhead County, Montana.

Fish Creek:(Clark) — North Fork of Salmon River in Idaho

Flathead — Misnomer for Salish Indians. Also, Salish sign language suggests flattening of sides of head.

Flathead River (Lewis and Clark) — Bitterroot River

Clark's River (Lewis) — Bitterroot River

Spitlem seukm (Salish/Flathead) — Bitterroot River

Flour Camp Creek — Warm Springs Creek, Ravalli County, Montana

Gap on Ridge of Rocky Mountains — Lewis and Clark Pass

Gates of the Rocky Mountains — A six-mile stretch of the Missouri River between Holter and and Houser dams north of Helena, Montana.

Gibbons Pass, also Neemeepoo Trail — Southeastern trail between Sula and Big Hole Basin across Continental Divide, Montana

Glade Creek in Idaho — Pack Creek, east of Lolo Pass

Glade Creek in Montana	Trail Creek: A branch of Wisdom River (Big Hole River), Beaverhead County.
Head of Glade Creek	Gibbon's Pass, on Continental Divide between Beaverhead and Ravalli Counties in Montana.
Hellgate River (Lewis and Clark)	Clark Fork River east of mouth of Bitterroot River
Hote Spring	Lolo Hot Springs
Ibex, also Angalia	Mountain or bighorn sheep.
Indian Medicine Tree	Sacred site of the Salish.
Isquit-co-qualla	"The Road to the Buffalo"
Jim Hell Rock	Huge rock named after Delaware Jim which blocked passage along the Flathead (Bitterroot) River
Konah (Shoshone)	Bitterroot flower
Kooskooski River	Clearwater River, Idaho.
Lolo	Indian word meaning "muddy water."
Lewis River	Snake or Salmon River.
Lolo Hot Springs	Hot water bubbles from huge granite rock, Lolo, Montana.
Medicine River (Lewis)	Sun River, Montana
Middle Fork of Clark River	East Fork of the Bitterroot River
West Fork of Clark's River	West Fork of the Bitterroot
Maria's River (named by Lewis)	Marias River, Montana
Minetares or Minnatares	Indian tribes: Piegan Blackfeet, Atsina, Hidatasas.
Montana (Spanish)	"Mountainous" Other names: Treasure State, Land of the Shining Mountains, Big Sky Country.
Moraine	Deposit of glacial fill
"Mush of Cows: (Clark)	Reconstituted dried cous root cake.
Nee me poo Trail	Gibbon's Pass, Montana.
Nez Perce (French)	Tribe of Indians residing in Idaho. Some members practiced nose piercing.
Nez Perce Trail	Lolo Trail
Oat lash shoots or Oot-la-shoots	Band of Salish/Flathead Indians
Oat la shoot Valley	Ross' Hole near Sula, Montana
Packer Meadows	Lower end of Pack Creek
Pahkees	Piegan Blackfeet, enemies
Parched Corn	Prepared dried corn kernels pressed; add water to eat.
Pogg a mogan (Chippewa)	Lewis;s name for Indian war club

Portable soup	A type of hardened bouillon gel used as base for soup.
Qoqa lx iskit (Nez Perce)	"Bison trail" Clark Fork River east of mouth of the Bitterroot River.
Quawmash	Camas plant, root used for food by Indians
Quawmash Flats	Wieppe Prairie
Quawmash Glades	Packer Meadows
Red Willow	Red osier dogwood
Roche Jaune (French)	Yellowstone River
Ross' Fork River	East Fork of the Bitterroot River
Saddle Mountain	Mountain west of Lost Trail Pass in Southwest Montana on Montana-Idaho border.
Sacgawea	Alternate spelling and pronunciation of Sacajawea.
Scannon	Seaman, Captain Lewis' Newfoundland dog.
Scattered Creek	Four channels of Burnt Fork Creek and possibly included Mill and North Spring Creek.
Shale spye	Salish scout
Shalees (Nez Perce)	Salish
Shields Creek	Headwaters southwest of Snake Nation (possible Campsite, September 3, 1805)
Skalkahoo (Salish)	Beaver
Snowey Mountain	Wendover Ridge
So yap pos (Nez Perce)	Members of the Corps of Discovery
Snake Nation	Shoshone Tribe
Spitlem suelken (Salish)	"The water of the bitterroot" (Bitterroot River)
Spitlemen (Salish)	"The place of the bitterroot" (Bitterroot Valley)
Spitlemen (Salish)	Bitterroot plant
Tatasiba (Shoshone)	"People with shaved heads": Salish/Flathead
Traveller's Rest Creek (Lewis and Clark)	Lolo Creek, LouLou,
Tumsumlech (Salish)	"No salmon" Lolo Creek
Tushepau	Tribal name of Salish/Flathead Indians.
Valley Plain River (Lewis)	East Fork of Clark's River (Clark Fork River now)
Weeping Child Creek	Translation of Indian name for Sleeping Child Creek.

Weippe Prairie	Quawmash (camas) flats
Welsh Indians	Myth about a tribe of Northwest Indians which were supposedly descendants of a Welsh traveller and were to have fair skin and an unusual dialect.
Werner's Creek	Clearwater River, Missoula County, Montana
Wisdom River	Big Hole River, Montana

LEWIS AND CLARK IN THE BITTERROOT
• *Footnotes* •

Chapter Two: OVER THE BITTERROOT RANGE TO ROSS' HOLE
1. Reuben Gold Thwaites, ed. *Original Journals of the Lewis and Clark Expedition 1805-1806* (New York: Dodd and Mead and Co. 1904-1905) vol. 3, p. 48.
2. Harry M. Majors, "Lewis and Clark Enter the Rocky Mountains," *Northwest Discovery,* vol. 7 (April and May, 1986) pp. 4-120 as quoted in *The Journals of the Lewis and Clark Expedition,* Gary Moulton, ed. (Lincoln: University of Nebraska Press, 1984) vol. 5, p. 186.
3. Moulton, vol. 9, p. 218.
4. Moulton, vol. 5, p. 183.
5. *Ibid.*p. 186.
6. Moulton, vol. 11, p. 300.

Chapter Three: MEMBERS OF THE EXPEDITION
1. Donald Jackson, ed. *"Letters of the Lewis and Clark expedition, with Related Documents: 1783-1854,* 2nd ed. (Urbana: University of Illinois Press, 1978) vol. I, pp. 57-60.
2. *Ibid.* pp. 110-111.
3. Bernard DeVoto, ed., *The Journals of Lewis and Clark,* (Boston: Houghton Mifflin Company, 1953) p. *li.*
4. *Ibid.* p. *lv.*
5. Moulton, vol. 11, p. *xv.*
6. Jackson, p. 369.

Chapter Four: MEETING THE SALISH
1. Moulton, vol. 5, p. 187.
2. *Ibid.*
3. Moulton, vol. 11, p. 302.
4. Olin D. Wheeler, *The Trail of Lewis and Clark 1804-1904* (New York: G. P. Putnams's Sons, 1926) vol. 2, p. 69.
5. Moulton, vol. 10, p. 138.
6. Moulton, vol. 11, p. 32.
7. Jackson, p. 64.
8. *Ibid., p. 61,12.*
9. Moulton, vol. 5, p. 196, 197.
10. *Moulton, vol. 4* p. 219.
11. Anderson, Virginia L. "Native Costumes of the Flathead and Kutenai Indian Tribes of the Flathead Indian Reservation of Montana. (a thesis) p. 45.
12. Moulton, vol. 5, p. 187.

13. Arlee, Johnny, "Over a Century of Moving to the Drum," Pablo, Montana: Salish-Kootenai College Press and Helena: Montana Historical Society, p. 27.

14. Peter Ronan. *Historical Sketch of the Flathead Nation* (Minneapolis: Russ and Haines Inc. 1890) p. 8,9.

15. Flathead Cultural Foundation, "A Brief History of the Flathead Tribe," p. 2

16. Merrill, Carolynne, "Culturally Scarred Trees," U.S. Forest Service Volunteer Researcher.

Jeff Hart, "Montana Early Plants and Native People." a lecture.

Mary Horstman, U.S. Forest Service Archeologist, Program Manager and Forest Historian, a field observation.

17. Moulton, vol. 5, p. 201.

18. Carol Lynn MacGregor, ed. *The Journals of Patrick Gass: Member of the Lewis and Clark Expedition.* (Missoula, Montana, Mountain Press Publishing Co., 1997) p.126.

19. Moulton, 5. p. 201

Chapter Six: THROUGH THE BITTERROOT VALLEY

1. Dr. Gene Swanzey, "High-Lights, July, 4, 1997.

2. Moulton, vol. 5, p. 189.

3. Swanzey, "High-Lights."

4. Moulton, vol. 11, p. 304

5. Stevensville Historical Writers, *Montana Genesis* (Missoula, Montana: Mountain Press Publishing Company, 1971), pp. 8-9.

6. Moulton, vol. 11, p. 301.

7. *Ibid.,* p. 305.

8. Moulton, vol. 5, p. 191.

9. Moulton, vol. 11, p. 305.

10. *Ibid.*

11. Moulton, vol. 10, p. 139.

12. Moulton, vol. 9, p. 221.

13. Ronan p. 15.

14. Swanzey, "High-Lights.

15. Moulton, vol. 5, p. 191.

16. *Ibid.*

17. Lucylle H. Evans, *St. Mary's in the Rocky Mountains, a History of the Cradle of Montana's Culture* (Stevensville, Montana: Montana Creative Consultants, 1975) p. 12.

18. Moulton, vol. 5, p. 193.

19. Thwaites, vol. 3, pp. 57-58.

20. *Ibid.* p. 58.

21. *Ibid.* p. 59.

22. Thwaites, vol. 7, p. 152.

Chapter Seven: DINING IN THE BITTERROOT

1. Moulton, vol. 11, p. 305.

2. Jackson, p. 217-18.

3. *Ibid.*, p. 81.

4. Eldon G. Chuinard, *Only One Man Died (Glendale, California: Arthur Clark Co., 1980) p. 160-162.*

5. *Ibid.* p. 161.

6. Jackson, p.78-85.

7. *Ibid.*, 94-95.

8. Thwaites, vol. 3, p. 339.

9. Moulton, vol. 7, p. 144.

10. *Thwaites, vol. 4. P. 331.*

11. Thwaites, vol. 3, p. 339.

12. Ambrose, p. 217.

13. Donald Barr Childsey, *Lewis and Clark: The Great Adventure* (New York: Crown Publishers, 1970) p. 100.

14. Dayton Duncan and Ken Burns, *The Journey of the Corps of Discovery, Lewis and Clark, an Illustrated History* (New York: Alfred A. Knopf, 1997) p. 152.

15. Moulton, vol. 5, p. 95.

16. Dan Cushman, *Cow Country Cookbook* (Santa Fe: Clear Light Publishers, 1993) p. 95.

17. Moulton, vol. 9 p. 217.

18. *Ibid.*, p. 218.

19. Moulton, vol. 5, p. 189.

20. *Ibid.*, p. 191.

21. Moulton, vol. 11, p. 315.

22 Moulton, vol. 10, p. 152.

23. *Ibid.* p. 245.

24. Thwaites, vol. 5 p. 246.

25. C. Leo Hitchcock and Arthur Cronquist *Flora of the Pacific Northwest* (Seattle: University of Washington Press, 1973) p. 309.

26. Thwaites, vol. 5 p. 12.

27. Thwaites, vol. 5, p. 111.

28. Thwaites vol. 5 p. 247.

Chapter Eight: THE NATURE OF THINGS

1. Richard Dillon, *Meriwether Lewis: A Biography* (New York: Coward-McCann, 1965) p.16.

2. Childsey, pp. 177-78.

3. Daniel B. Bodkin, *Our Natural History: The Lessons of Lewis and Clark* (New York: G.P. Putnam's Sons, 1995) pp. 129-130.

4. Thwaites, vol. 3, p. 13.

5. *Ibid.*

6. Moulton, vol. 8, p. 32.

7. *Ibid.* p.79.

8. Ambrose, p. 432.

9. Bitter Root Valley Historical Society, *Bitterroot Trails* (Hamilton, Montana:

Bitter Root Valley Historical Society, 1982), p. 18.

10. Dr. Dee Strickler, *Prairie Wildflowers* (Columbia Falls, Montana, 1986) p. 80.

11. Jerry DeSanto, *Bitterroot* (Babb, Montana: Lere Press, 1993) p. 3.

12. *Ibid.*

13, Bitter Root Valley Historical Society, p. 26.

14. Moulton, vol. 8.

15. Thwaites, vol. 3 p. 17.

16. *Ibid.* p. 44.

17. Paul Russell Cutright, *Lewis and Clark: Pioneering Naturalists* (Chicago: University of Illinois Press, 1969) p. 186.

18. Thwaites, vol. 5, p. 74.

19. Moulton, vol. 7, p. 348.

20. Roger Tory Peterson, *Peterson Field Guides: Western Birds* (New York, Houghton Mifflin Col., 1990) p. 222.

21. Cutright, p. 128.

22. Thwaites, vol. 3, p. 57.

23. Moulton, vol. 8.

24. Donald F. Nell and John E. Taylor, *Lewis and Clark in the Three Rivers Valleys* (Tucson, Arizona: The Patrice Press 1996) pp. 276-277.

25. Andrea Merrill and Judy Jacobson, *Montana Almanac* (Helena, Montana: Falcon Publishing Company, Inc., 1997), p. 28.

26. Moulton, vol. 8, p. 79, 80.

27. Thwaites, vol. 3, p. 57.

28. Moulton, vol. 8.

29. Thwaites, vol. 3, p. 57.

30. Moulton, vol. 5, p. 203.

31. Moulton, vol. 10, p. 141.

32. Thwaites, vol. 5, p. 172.

33. Ronald V. Loge, M.D., "Two doses of Bark and Opium: Lewis and Clark as Physicians" *We Proceeded On, vol. 23,* no. 1, p. 14.

34. Chuinard, p. 271.

Chapter Nine: TRAVELLER'S REST 1805

1. Moulton, vol. 5. 196.

2. Private interview with Pat Deschamps, property owner, February 21, 1998.

Chapter Ten: OVER THE LOLO TRAIL WESTWARD

1. Thwaites, vol. 7, p. 153.

2. Ralph Space, *The Lolo Trail: A History of Events Connected with the Lolo Trail Since Lewis and Clark* (Lewiston, Idaho: Printcraft Printing, 1984) p. 27.

3. Moulton, vol. 10, p. 141.

4. Thwaites, vol. 3, p. 63.

5. Moulton, vol. 5, p. 203.

6. Thwaites, vol. 3, p. 69.

7. *Ibid.*, p. 72.
8. Moulton, vol. 5, p. 214.
9. *Ibid.,* p. 211.
10. Thwaites, vol. 3, p. 100.

Chapter Eleven: THE RETURN TO THE BITTERROOT—1806.
1. Moulton, vol. 7, p. 197.
2. Joseph A. Mussulman, "The Greatest Harmony, 'Medicine Songs on the Lewis and Clark Trail,'" *We Proceeded On,* vol 23, no 4, pp-410.
3. Moulton, vol. 8, pp. 25-26.
4. *Ibid.,* vol 7, pp. 226.
5. *Ibid.,* p. 229.
6. *Ibid.,* p. 278.
7. Ambrose, p. 369.
8. Ibid.
9. Moulton, vol. 8, p. 25, 26.
10. *Ibid.,* p. 29.
11. *Ibid.,* p. 31.
12. *Ibid.,* p. 34.
13. Space, p. 33.
14. Moulton, vol. 8, p. 37.
15. *Ibid.,* p. 66.
16. Thwaites, vol. 5, p. 173.

Chapter Twelve: TRAVELLER'S REST—1806
1. Moulton, vol. 8, p. 68.
2. Swanzey, "High-Lights".
3. Moulton, vol. 8, p. 79.
4. *Ibid.*

Chapter Thirteen: RETRACING THE BITTERROOT VALLEY—JULY 1806
1. Moulton, vol. 8, p. 83.
2. Thwaites, vol. 5, p. 245.
3. Ibid., p. 245, 246.
4. *Ibid.*
5. *Ibid.*
6. Moulton, vol. 10, p. 109.
7. Thwaites, vol. 5, p. 249.
8. *Ibid.*
9. Ibid. p. 249-250.
10. Elliot Coues, ed. *The History of the Lewis and Clark Expedition* (New York: Reprint by Dover Publications, vol. III,   p. 1122.
11. K. Ross Toole, *Montana, An Uncommon Land* (Norman: University of Oklahoma Press, 1959) p. 39.

Chapter Fourteen: CLARK-BITTERROOT TO YELLOWSTONE

1. James P. Ronda, *Lewis and Clark Among the Indians* (Lincoln: University of Nebraska Press, 1984), p. 255.
2. Moulton, vol. 8, p. 115.
3. K. Ross Toole, p. 55.
4. Moulton, vol. 8, p. 175.
5. *Ibid.* p. 173.
6. Toole, p. 69.
7. Moulton, vol. 8, p. 180.
8. Coues, vol III, p. 1134.
9. Moulton, vol. 8, p. 190.

Chapter Fifteen: THE LAST LEG, August-September 1806

1. Moulton, vol. 8, p. 364.
2. Thwaites, vol. 5, p. 395.

LEWIS AND CLARK IN THE BITTERROOT
• *Bibliography* •

Ambrose, Stephen E. *Undaunted Courage: Meriwether Lewis, Thomas Jefferson and the Opening of the American West.* New York: Simon and Schuster, 1996.

Anderson, Virginia L., master thesis "Native Costumes of the Flathead and Kutenai Indian Tribes of the Flathead Indian Reservation in Montana", Kansas State College, 1957.

Andrews, Ralph W. *Curtis Western Indians, Life and Works of Edward S. Curtis.* New York: Bonanza Books, 1962.

Arlee, Johnny, *Over a Century of Moving to the Drum: Salish Indian Celebrations on the Flathead Indian Reservation.* Pablo, Montana: Salish Kootenai College Press and Helena, Montana: Montana Historical Society, 1998.

Bergantino, Robert. "Lewis and Clark in the Bitterroot Valley".

Betts, Robert B., *In Search of York.* Boulder, Colorado: Associated University Press, 1985.

Bitter Root Valley *Historical* Society. *Bitterroot Trails.* Hamilton, Montana: BRVHS, 1982.

Boaz, Franz and Teit, James. "Coeur D'Alene, Flathead and Okanogan Indians". reprint. Fairfield, Washington: Ye Galleon Press, 1965.

Bodkin, Daniel B. *Our Natural History: The Lessons of Lewis and Clark.* New York: BG.P. Putnam's Sons, 1995.

Burk, Dale A., *A Brush With The West*, Stoneydale Press Publishing Company, Stevensville, Montana, 1978.

Burnham, Patricia M. "Russell and the Capitol Mural," *Montana History: The Magazine of the Montana Historical Society.*

Campbell, Charles V. "Westward Barriers Guidebook for Routes Followed by Lewis and Clark Across the Rocky Mountains in 1805-6."
Missoula Traveler's Rest Chapter, Lewis and Clark Trail Heritage Foundation, 1994

Childsey, Donald Barr. *Lewis and Clark: The Great Adventure*, New York: Crown Publishers, 1970.

Chuinard, Eldon G. *Only One Man Died: Medical Aspects of the Lewis and Clark Expedition.* Glendale, California: Arthur Clark Co. 1980

Clark, Charles G. *The Men of the Lewis and Clark Expedition and a Composite Diary of their Activities.* Glendale, California: The Arthur H. Clark Company, 1970.

Clark, W.A. *The Indian Sign Language with Brief Explanatory Notes.* Philadelphia: L.R. Hammerly & Co., 1885.

Cous, Elliott, ed., *History of the Expedition Under the Command of Lewis and Clark.* New York: Dover Publications, reprint three volumes, 1965.

Cushman, Dan. *Cow Country Cookbook.* Santa Fe: Clear Light Publishers, 1992.

Cutright, Paul. *Lewis and Clark: Pioneering Naturalist,* Lincoln: University of Nebraska Press, 1969.

Davis, Barbara A. *Edward S. Curtis: the Life and Times of a Shadow Catcher.* San Francisco, Chronicle Books, 1985.

DeSanto, Jerry. *Bitterroot.* Babb, Montana: Lere Press, 1993

DeVoto, Bernard, ed., *The Journals of Lewis and Clark.* Boston: Houghton, Mifflin Company, Riverside Press, Cambridge, 1953.

Dillon, Richard. *Meriwether Lewis: A Biography.* New York: Coward, McCann, 1965.

Duncan, Dayton, "What the Lewis & Clark Expedition Means to America," *We Proceeded On* vol. 23, no. 3 (August, 1997).

Duncan, Dayton and Ken Burns. *The Journey of the Corps of Discovery, Lewis and Clark, an Illustrated History.* New York: Alfred A. Knopf, 1997.

Evans, Lucylle H. *St. Mary's in the Rocky Mountains, A History of the Cradle of Montana's Culture.* Stevensville, Montana: Creative Consultants, 1975.

Ewers, John C. *The Horse in the Blackfoot Indian Culture, with Comparative Materials from Other Western Tribes.* Washington, D.C.: Smithsonian Institution Press, 1955.

Fahey, John. *The Flathead Indians.* Norman: University of Oklahoma Press, 1974.

Ferris, Robert G. and Appleman, Roy. *Lewis and Clark: Historic Places Associated with their Transcontinental Exploration, 1804-1806.* Washington, D.C.: United States Department of the Interior, National Park Service, 1975.

Flathead Cultural Foundation. *A Brief History of the Flathead Tribes.* St. Ignatius, Montana, 1993.

Gustafson, R.W. *Seaman: The Dog Who Helped Explore America.* Stevensville, Montana, Stoneydale Press Publishing Company, 1998.

Hitchcock, C. Leo and Cronquist, Arthur. *Flora of the Pacific Northwest.* Seattle: University of Washington Press, 1973.

Hosmer, James K., LL.D., *History of the Expedition of Captains Lewis & Clark, 1804-5-6.* Vol. 1. Chicago: A.C. McClurg & Co., 1924.

Hoxie, Frederick E., ed. *Encyclopedia of North American Indians.* Boston and New York: Houghton Mifflin Co., 1996.

Hungry Wolf, Adolf and Beverly. *Indian Tribes of the Northern Rockies.* Summertown, Tennessee: Book Publishing Company, 1989.

Jackson, Donald. ed., *Letters of the Lewis and Clark Expedition, with Related Documents:* 1783-1854, 2nd ed. Urbana: University of Illinois Press, 1978.

Johnson, Olga Weydemeyer. *Flathead and Kootenay: The Rivers, the Tribes and the Region's Traders.* Glendale, California: The Arthur H. Clark Company, 1969.

Lavender, David. *The Way to the Western Sea.* New York: Harper and Rowe, 1988.

Loge, Ronald V. M.D. "'Two doses of bark and opium': Lewis and Clark As Physicians," *We Proceeded On.* vol. 23, no. 1.

Large, Arlen J. "Expedition Specialists—The Talented Helpers of Lewis & Clark." *We Proceeded On,* vol. 20, no. 1 (February, 1994).

MacGregor, Carol Lynn, ed. *The Journals of Patrick Gass: Member of the Lewis and Clark Expedition.* Missoula, Montana: Mountain Press Publishing Co., 1997.

Merrill, Andrea and Jaccobson, Judy. *Montana Almanac* .Helena Montana: Falcon Publishing Co., 1997.

Moulton, Gary, ed. *The Journals of the Lewis and Clark Expedition.* Lincoln: University of Nebraska Press, 1988.

Mussulman, Joseph A. "The Greatest Harmony: Medicine Songs on the Lewis and Clark Trail."
We Proceeded On vol. 23, no. 4 (November, 1997).

Nell, Donald F. and Taylor, John E. *Lewis and Clark in the Three Rivers Valleys.* Tucson, Arizona: The Patrice Press, 1996.

Pearson, T.G. *Birds of America.* Garden City: Doubleday and Company, 1917.

Peterson, Jacqueline with Peer, Laura. *Sacred Encounters: Father DeSmet and the Indians of the Rocky Mountain West.* Norman and London: Washington State University in association with University of Oklahoma Press, 1993.

Peterson, Roger Tory. *Peterson Field Guides: Western Birds.* New York: Houghton Mifflin Company, 1990.

Robbins, Chandler S., Bertel Bruun and Herber S. Zim. *A Guide to Field Identification: Birds of North America.* New York: Golden Press, 1966.

Ronan, Peter. *Historical Sketch of the Flathead Nation.* Minneapolis: Russ and Haines, Inc., 1890.

Ronda, James P. *Lewis and Clark Among the Indians.* Lincoln: University of Nebraska Press, 1984.

Snyder, George. *In the Footsteps of Lewis and Clark.* National Geographic Staff, 1970.

Space, Ralph. *The Lolo Trail: A History of Events Connected with the Lolo Trail Since Lewis and Clark.* Lewiston, Idaho: Idaho Printcraft Printing, 1984.

Steffen, Jerome O. *William Clark: Jeffersonian Man on the Frontier.* Norman: University of Oklahoma, 1977.

Stevensville Historical Society, *Montana Genesis,* Missoula: Mountain Press Publishing Company, 1971.

Strickler, Dr. Dee. *Prairie Wildflowers.* Columbia Falls, Montana, 1986.

Swanzey, Dr. Gene. "High-Lites of the Bitterroot: *Hi-Lites,* 1997.

Toole, K. Ross, *Montana: An Uncommon Land.* Norman: University of Oklahoma Press, 1959.

Thwaites, Reuben G. ed. *Original Journals of the Lewis and Clark Expedition.* New York: Dodd and Mead and Company, 1804-05.

Wetmore, Alexander. *Song and Garden Birds of North America.* Washington D.C.: National Geographic Society, 1964.

Wheeler, Olin D. *The Trail of Lewis and Clark, 1804-1806.* New York: G. P. Putnam and Sons, 1916. vol. 2.

Wissler, Clark *Indians of the United States.* New York: Anchor Books, 1966.

INDEX

LISTING OF BOOKS

Additional copies of **LEWIS AND CLARK IN THE BITTERROOT,** *and many other of Stoneydale Press' books on outdoor recreation, regional history, or historical reminisces centered around the Northern Rocky Mountain region, are available at many book stores and sporting goods stores, or direct from Stoneydale Press. If you'd like more information, you can contact us by calling a Toll Free number,* **1-800-735-7006,** *or by writing the address at the bottom of the page. Here's a partial listing of some of the books that are available:*

Historical Reminisces/Other

Seaman: The Dog Who Helped Explore America, *By R. W. "Rib" Gustafson, 70 pages, softcover, in text and illustration, a children's perspective on Seaman, the Newfoundland Retriever that accompanied the Lewis and Clark Expedition on its epic journey.*

Indian Trails & Grizzly Tales, *By Bud Cheff Sr., 212 pages, available in clothbound and softcover editions.*

They Left Their Tracks, *By Howard Copenhaver, Recollections of Sixty Years as a Wilderness Outfitter, 192 pages, clothbound or softcover editions (One of our all-time most popular books.)*

More Tracks, *By Howard Copenhaver, 78 Years of Mountains, People & Happiness, 180 pages, clothbound or softcover editions.*

Copenhaver Country, *By Howard Copenhaver. A delightful collection of stories from out of the Ovando, Montana, and Bob Marshall Wilderness areas in Montana by a noted storyteller, 160 pages, clothbound and softcover editions.*

Mules & Mountains, *By Margie E. Hahn, the story of Walt Hahn, Forest Service Packer, 164 pages, clothbound or softcover editions.*

Montana's Mineral County In Retrospect, *By Margie E. Hahn, historical look at rich ·history of western-most part of Montana, many historical photographs, 160 pages, softcover only.*

A Brush With The West, *By Dale A. Burk, 140 pages, clothbound, perspective on role of art on historical and contemporary perspectives of place in the West and the Northern Rockies.*

New Interpretations, *By Dale A. Burk, 204 pages, softcover, insightful third edition of development of western art in Montana from the time of Russell and Seltzer into the late 1960s.*

Mules Across The Great Wide Open, *By Jody Foss, 288 pages, compelling narrative by Jody Foss on trip by mules she, her sister, and another companion made from Park City, Utah, north into Wyoming and then across Montana and Idaho into eastern Washington.*

Outdoor Books

The Elk Mystique, By Mike Lapinski, large format book of color photographs and text about the history and mystique of the wapiti, the American elk by one of nation's top outdoor writers. A gorgeous all-color book with many photos of elk in the wild.

Self Defense For Nature Lover, By Mike Lapinski. Subtitled "Handling Dangerous Situations With Wild Critters," this timely and helpful book is a detailed guide to self defense in terms of potential outdoors dangers involving mountain lions, grizzly bears, black bears, etc.

The Woodsman and His Hatchet, By Bud Cheff, Eighty years on back country survival by an expert whose secrets of common sense wilderness survival are described in detail, 112 pages, softcover only.

So You Really Want To Be a Guide, By Dan Cherry. The latest and single most authoritative source on what it takes to be a guide today. This book is an excellent guideline to a successful guiding career. Softcover edition only.

Field Care Handbook For The Hunter & Fisherman, By Bill Sager & Duncan Gilchrist, 168 pages, comb binding, many photographs and illustrations. The most comprehensive field care handbook available.

Cookbooks

Camp Cookbook, Featuring Recipes for Fixing Both at Home and in Camp, With Field Stories by Dale A. Burk, 216 pages, comb binding

Cooking for Your Hunter, By Miriam Jones, 180 pages, comb binding

That Perfect Batch: The Hows & Whys of Making Sausage and Jerky, By Clem Stechelin, 116 pages, comb binding.

Venison As You Like It, By Ned Dobson. This book covers the details for utilizing wild game in roasts, steaks, hamburger, chili, chops, casseroles, sausages, etc. Over 200 recipes.

STONEYDALE PRESS PUBLISHING COMPANY
523 Main Street • Box 188
Stevensville, Montana 59870
Phone: 406-777-2729